The Llandudno & Colwyn Bay Electric Railway

by
Keith Turner

THE OAKWOOD PRESS

First Edition 1993
Second Edition 2007

British Library Cataloguing in Publication Data
A Record for this book is available from the British Library
ISBN 978 0 85361 668 9

Typeset by Oakwood Graphics.
Repro by PKmediaworks, Cranborne, Dorset.
Printed by Progressive Print Services, Kidderminster, Worcs.

A general view of the Promenade at Llandudno, looking towards the Great Orme, capturing the grandeur and elegance of the seafront buildings. *Oakwood Collection*

Front cover: Service car No. 13 (ex-Bournemouth) in the loop at Hooson's Corner, alongside toastrack No. 21 on the 1951 Light Railway Transport League special working.
D.W.K. Jones

Rear cover, top: No. 1 (ex-Accrington) in Bryn-y-Bia Road, ascending the Little Orme from Badafon Fields in May 1951.
D.W.K. Jones

Rear cover, bottom: Toastrack No. 21 about to descend Penrhyn Hill, on an enthusiasts' special.
D.W.K. Jones

Published by The Oakwood Press (Usk), P.O. Box 13, Usk, Mon., NP15 1YS.
E-mail: sales@oakwoodpress.co.uk
Website: www.oakwoodpress.co.uk

Contents

	Introduction to First Edition	5
	Introduction to Second Edition	5
Chapter One	A Matter of Some Doubt	7
Chapter Two	Open at Last	15
Chapter Three	The Route Described	27
Chapter Four	Expansion…	43
Chapter Five	…and Contraction	53
Chapter Six	World War II and After	67
Chapter Seven	Closure	81
Chapter Eight	Epilogue	93
Chapter Nine	Operations	101
Chapter Ten	Rolling Stock	113
Appendix One	Fleet List	153
Appendix Two	Fleet List of the Buses	155
Appendix Three	The Seaton Connection	156
Appendix Four	Other Tramway Proposals	157
	Acknowledgements	158
	Bibliography	159
	Index	160

Service car No. 5 (ex-Accrington) on 21st May, 1951 in Gloddaeth Street loop before Hooson's Corner, passing toastrack 21 on a special working for members of the Light Railway Transport League.

D.W.K. Jones

432 - Llandudno - Craig - Y - don and Llandudno

An early postcard view of almost the whole of Llandudno, with the West Shore on the extreme left, the Great Orme in the centre and Ormes Bay and Craig-y-don on the right. The sweep of Mostyn Broadway, still scarcely encroached upon, is clearly visible in the middle distance.

Author's Collection

Introduction to First Edition

North Wales was an area rich in tramway schemes but poor in actual lines. Of the few that were constructed, probably the most famous is the Great Orme Tramway, if only for the reason that it still operates today. The second most famous, and undoubtedly of more interest to the tramway enthusiast, was one that also served Llandudno: the Llandudno & Colwyn Bay Electric Railway. Despite its title it was a tramway, not a railway, and of all the North Wales tramways it had the longest route mileage, the largest car fleet and, at the outset, the greatest problems. How it overcame those, and what happened thereafter, is the subject matter of the following pages.

This account is based primarily on the relevant sections of the author's *North Wales Tramways*, published in 1979 but for several years now out of print. For this history the opportunity has been taken to expand the narrative at several points where further information has come to light, to increase greatly the number of photographic and other illustrations and, wherever relevant, to bring the story up to date.

Introduction to Second Edition

The year 2007 marks the centenary of the opening of the Llandudno & Colwyn Bay Electric Railway, and it is fitting that this history of this much-loved tramway, still fondly remembered by a generation of holiday-makers, should be reissued at this time. Since the first edition appeared more than a decade ago further historical and technical details of the line have come to light, and the opportunity has been taken to amend and expand the account as appropriate - even though this has meant that the previously-accepted version of exactly which tramcars were renumbered what and when has had to be changed accordingly.

The story has also been updated with respect to possible future developments for in recent years the Llandudno & Colwyn Bay Tramway Society has gone from strength to strength and - *see Chapter Eight* - the question is now not 'Will the trams ever return to Llandudno?' as suggested in the first edition, but 'When?'

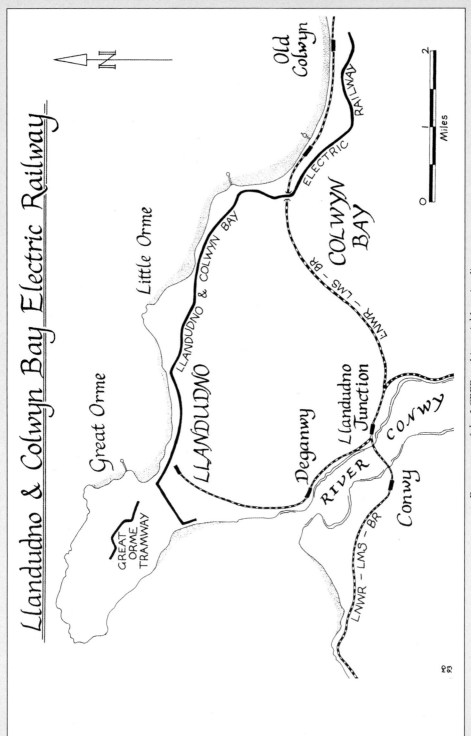

Route map of the LCBER and its neighbouring lines.

Chapter One

A Matter of Some Doubt

The early history of the Llandudno & Colwyn Bay Electric Railway (LCBER) is convoluted in the extreme and, if set out in full detail, would more than fill this book several times over. Much of the tramway's lengthy promotion story is, quite frankly, exceedingly boring - and has been so ever since it ceased to be of relevance to those directly concerned in the events of the dozen or so years spanning the turn of the 20th century. What follows in this chapter and the next is a potted version of the promotional aspirations, squabbles and setbacks that preceded the opening of the line; by presenting only the main and ultimately relevant events (and non-events!) it is hoped that a far clearer account of what took place during this period can be achieved.

As anyone who has visited the town will know, the most distinctive feature of Llandudno is the Great Orme; indeed, before the modern town was laid out, it was about the only distinctive feature of the area. From the west, as far along the coast as Bangor, it appears to be an off-shore island rising abruptly from the sea (to a height of 679 ft); it is in fact a limestone mass somes two miles long and one mile wide with steep cliffs on three sides but on the fourth - the southern side - it is connected by a very low, very flat strip of land to the rest of the mainland. St Tudno's church on the Orme's comparatively level summit gave its name to the parish (Llandudno in Welsh meaning 'the church of Tudno') and originally served the few miners' cottages huddled together for shelter on the landward side. As late as the mid-19th century these and two small inns were the only habitations on the peninsula, then part of the estate of Edward, the 1st Baron Mostyn.

By this date North Wales was already becoming 'tourist conscious' and Mostyn realised that the rise of the fashionable watering-place need by no means be confined to the south coast of England; with this in mind he began his grand scheme, not only to build from scratch a complete resort but then to elevate it to a position in the North equal to that held by Brighton in the South. Accordingly, in 1843 Mostyn secured an Enclosure Act for the area (steered through Parliament by his son and heir the Hon. Edward Mostyn Lloyd-Mostyn, MP for Flintshire) and six years later offered and sold 176 plots of land on the low-lying peninsula; the scheme had taken its first steps towards becoming an unqualified success fulfilling all of Mostyn's hopes.

So sprang up the town that exists today, facing out to the north-east across the sands of Ormes Bay with the Great Orme on the left and its smaller namesake to the east, the Little Orme, on the right. With its broad promenade and majestic sweep of hotels and boarding houses along the bay it followed rigidly the pattern of its day, but in one important respect it was unique - and that one respect was without doubt one of the principal reasons behind Llandudno's success: behind the town was another beach - a longer, wider, more desolate stretch of sand bordering the Conwy estuary. This added attraction (and the splendid views from it), together with the impressive majesty of the Great

LIGHT RAILWAYS ACT, 1896.

LLANDUDNO AND COLWYN BAY LIGHT RAILWAY ORDER, 1898.

ORDER

MADE BY THE

LIGHT RAILWAY COMMISSIONERS,

AND MODIFIED AND CONFIRMED BY THE

BOARD OF TRADE,

AUTHORISING THE CONSTRUCTION OF

LIGHT RAILWAYS FROM COLWYN BAY TO LLANDUDNO IN THE COUNTIES OF DENBIGH AND CARNARVON.

Presented to both Houses of Parliament by Command of Her Majesty.

LONDON:
PRINTED FOR HER MAJESTY'S STATIONERY OFFICE,
BY DARLING & SON, LTD., 1–3, GREAT ST. THOMAS APOSTLE, E.C.

And to be purchased, either directly or through any Bookseller, from
EYRE & SPOTTISWOODE, EAST HARDING STREET, FLEET STREET, E.C.; and
32, ABINGDON STREET, WESTMINSTER, S.W.; or
JOHN MENZIES & Co., 12, HANOVER STREET, EDINBURGH, and
90, WEST NILE STREET, GLASGOW; or
HODGES, FIGGIS, & Co., LIMITED, 104, GRAFTON STREET, DUBLIN.

1899.

[C. 9395.]   Price 3d.

Title page of the LCBER's 1898 Light Railway Order.

Orme, meant that Mostyn's project could hardly fail and by 1877 had been dubbed 'the Queen of Welsh watering-places' in the guidebooks of the time. In 1881 Llandudno's population was 4,193 and by 1891 it had grown by nearly half as much again to 6,065; 10 years later it had become an Urban District (in 1895, principally by absorbing its neighbouring Civil Parish of Eglwys Rhos) with a total of 9,279 inhabitants - a figure which could probably be safely doubled, or even tripled, any time during the summer months). So Llandudno has grown to this day, to more than twice the 1901 figure: purely residential, relying completely and utterly on its annual surfeit of holiday-makers and conference-goers to the total exclusion of any other significant form of industry apart from the necessary services needed to cater for inhabitants and visitors alike.

Less than five miles along the coast to the south-east, past the Little Orme, the township of Colwyn Bay experienced a similar boom in the wake of Llandudno's ascension. A century ago the town was virtually non-existent; what settlement there was in the area was centred around the villages of Colwyn (now Old Colwyn), a short distance inland to the east, and Llandrillo-yn-Rhos, similarly situated to the west. By 1887, though, it had developed sufficiently as a resort in Llandudno's wake to warrant being placed under a Local Board as a local government area in its own right; the 1891 census returned a population of 4,754 and four years later the Colwyn Bay & Colwyn Urban District Council was incorporated. In 1901 the population was not far behind that of Llandudno at 8,689 and the town was growing rapidly, swallowing up as suburbs Old Colwyn, and Llandrillo-yn-Rhos and its adjacent headland at the northern end of the long, curving bay from which the new town took its name, midway between Old Colwyn and the Little Orme. (As Llandrillo-yn-Rhos spread out to the coast, the headland area became known as Rhos-on-Sea, this name coming in later years to encompass the older settlement.)

Contemporary with the promotion of the cable-worked Great Orme Tramway up that headland in the 1880s and 1890s as part tourist amenity, part local transport service, was the idea of linking Llandudno with Colwyn Bay by a direct tramway or light railway. The London & North Western Railway (LNWR) provided only a rather roundabout route between the two via its Llandudno branch line (opened 1858) to Llandudno Junction and thence along its main Chester-Holyhead line (opened 1848) to Colwyn Bay. A more direct route would also have had the advantage of passing through the principal built-up areas avoided by the railway, thus tapping potential traffic at source. This idea was first mooted during the early 1890s, gaining momentum as a result of the 1896 Light Railways Act (which made the whole process of obtaining the necessary authorization considerably cheaper than previously had been the case).

Things now started to move quickly: interested local parties, headed by George Griffiths, applied in December 1896 for a Light Railway Order to construct 4½ miles of 3 ft 6 in. gauge electric tramway between the towns at an estimated cost of over £28,000; the application, heard at Colwyn Bay on 23rd February, 1897, was rejected on the grounds that the interests of the local landowners and Llandudno Council had not been sufficiently considered.

Llandudno's first tramway was the Great Orme Tramway. This is the lower section of the line, on a bright sunny day shortly after its 1902 opening, looking across the bay to the Little Orme.   *Author's Collection*

Undaunted by this setback, the promoters made their next move on 9th May of the same year when the Light Railway & General Construction Co. Ltd (LR&GCCo.) was registered, to construct the proposed line, with a nominal capital of 75,000 Ordinary shares and an equal number of 6 per cent Cumulative Preference shares. The four Directors were J. Eckersley, D.R. Gibb, E. Hewitt and T.H. Fitzsimmons; the Secretary was John Morris and the registered office in Manchester. At the same time company applied to the Light Railway Commissioners for the necessary Light Railway Order, the Directors and proprietors meeting to approve the draft document on 30th August. The application this time was for authorization for a much grander scheme of 8 miles 25.45 chains of light railway, as one line, from the eastern end of Bay View Road at the corner of Greenfield Road in Colwyn Bay, over Penrhyn Hill (the landward side of the Little Orme), through Llandudno town centre and thence southwards to Deganwy railway station on the LNWR's Llandudno branch at the mouth of the Conwy estuary. The gauge proposed was still 3 ft 6 in., with the tramway to be worked by animal power (i.e. horse) or electricity. The estimated cost for this much longer line was just over £65,000.

The public enquiry into the application was held by the Commissioners in Colwyn Bay on 12th November, 1897; their decision was deferred until a second sitting on 18th May, 1898 on account of the declared opposition of Llandudno UDC, which body had made an application for a Board of Trade Provisional Tramway Order to construct part of the proposed line (2 miles 65 chains) itself; in April 1898 however the UDC dropped its own scheme in favour of the company's. The Commissioners decided in favour of the LR&GCCo. and their approval was confirmed on 2nd June, 1899 by the Board of Trade in the shape of the Llandudno and Colwyn Bay Light Railway Order, 1898. (It should perhaps be pointed out here that although nominally an electric railway and legally a light railway, the Llandudno & Colwyn Bay Electric Railway has always been commonly regarded as a tramway - which, in all other respects, it was!)

In addition to the above-mentioned proposals, the following points are especially important since this Order provided the basis for the subsequent eventual construction of the tramway: three years were allowed for the compulsory purchase of the land needed and for the completion of the works, electric traction was permitted and, under Section 76 of the Order, the sum of £2,980 had to be paid into court by the company before it could exercise its powers. (Section 77 provided for the repayment of this deposit when the line was opened.) Powers for compulsory purchase of the concern were given to the three local authorities involved: after 28 years for Llanduno UDC and after 25 years for Colwyn Bay UDC and Conway RDC.

This initial flurry of activity over, the scheme entered a new phase of procrastination, promises and pleading that lasted five years before anything concrete was achieved. At the bottom of it all was a simple matter of time and money - or, more correctly, a lack of those two commodities. Legal and other costs had amounted to £17,000 by the end of 1899; two years later that sum had risen to £25,000 (by which time the company's registered office had moved to Bush House, Bush Lane, London EC). As the raising of the capital proved a slower process than had been originally envisaged, so the company was forced to spend money in purchasing time extensions just to retain its powers. Nor was the situation helped by the attitude of those who were in a position to speed up the proceedings. As the *Caernarvon & Denbigh Herald* of 23rd August, 1901 declared in a leader article:

> The petulant obstruction, the policy of opposition by the council, the exorbitant demands of Lord Mostyn, and the thousand and one claims made by adjacent local authorities nearly defeated the promotion of the movement by piling on heavy floating expenditure.

Under the 1898 Order the date for completion was 2nd June, 1902; with nothing at all begun the company - now entitled the Llandudno, Colwyn Bay, and Rhyl [!] Electric Traction Co. Ltd (LCB&RETCo.) - applied in November 1901 for an extension of time. The Light Railway Commissioners held their enquiry in Colwyn Bay on 5th March, 1902 and approved both this application and one for a 52.75-chain deviation within Colwyn Bay. This provided a different route from Rhos-on-Sea up Rhos Road and across the fields, skirting rather than crossing the estate of Sir George Cayley (who had unsuccessfully opposed this portion of the authorized route in 1898), before rejoining the 1898 route over the LNWR main line and down Princes Road, passing close to Colwyn Bay railway station before terminating at the eastern end of Bay View Road. In June, while awaiting the Board of Trade's confirmation of the Order, the company finally paid into court the £2,980 specified in Section 76 of the 1898

SCHEDULE.

MAXIMUM RATES AND CHARGES FOR GOODS MATERIALS ARTICLES AND THINGS CONVEYED BY THE COMPANY ON THE RAILWAYS.

Animals.

For every horse mule or other beast of draught or burden fourpence per head per mile ;

For every ox cow bull or head of cattle threepence per head per mile :

For calves pigs sheep and small animals one penny halfpenny per head per mile.

Goods.

For all coals coke culm charcoal cannel limestone chalk lime salt sand fireclay cinders dung compost and all sorts of manure and all undressed materials for the repair of public roads or highways twopence per ton per mile ;

For all iron ironstone iron ore pig iron bar iron rod iron sheet iron hoop iron plates of iron slabs billets and rolled iron bricks slag and stone stones for building pitching and paving tiles slates and clay (except fireclay) and for wrought iron not otherwise specially classed herein and for heavy iron castings including railway chairs twopence halfpenny per ton per mile ;

For all sugar grain corn flour hides dye woods earthenware timber staves deals and metals (except iron) nails anvils vices and chains and for light iron castings threepence per ton per mile :

For cotton wools drugs manufactured goods and all other wares merchandise fish articles matters or things not otherwise specially classed herein fourpence per ton per mile :

For every carriage of whatever description one shilling per mile.

Small Parcels.

For any parcel not exceeding seven pounds in weight threepence ;

For any parcel exceeding seven pounds and not exceeding fourteen pounds in weight fivepence ;

For any parcel exceeding fourteen pounds and not exceeding twenty-eight pounds in weight sevenpence ;

For any parcel exceeding twenty-eight pounds and not exceeding fifty-six pounds in weight ninepence ;

For any parcel exceeding fifty-six pounds but not exceeding five hundred pounds in weight such sum as the Company may think fit ;

Provided that articles sent in large aggregate quantities although made up in separate parcels such as bags of sugar coffee meal and the like shall not be deemed small parcels but that term shall apply only to single parcels in separate packages.

Single Articles of Great Weight.

The Company shall not be bound to carry single articles of great weight but if they do carry such articles they may charge :—

For the carriage of any iron boiler cylinder or single piece of machinery or single piece of timber or stone or other single article the weight of which including the carriage shall exceed four tons but shall not exceed eight tons such sum as the Company may think fit not exceeding two shillings per ton per mile ;

For the carriage of any single piece of timber stone machinery or other single article the weight of which with the carriage shall exceed eight tons such sum as the Company may think fit.

Regulations as to Rates.

For animals goods or things conveyed on the railways for any less distance than two miles the Company may demand rates and charges as for two miles ;

In computing the said rates and charges a fraction of a mile shall be deemed a mile ;

For the fraction of a ton the Company may demand rates according to the number of quarters of a ton in such fraction and if there be a fraction of a quarter of a ton such fraction shall be deemed a quarter of a ton ;

With respect to all articles except stone and timber the weight shall be determined according to the imperial avoirdupois weight ;

With respect to stone and timber fourteen cubic feet of stone forty cubic feet of oak mahogany teak beech or ash and fifty cubic feet of any other timber shall be deemed one ton weight and so in proportion for any smaller quantity ;

In the case of goods and single articles of great weight the Company may demand such charges as are reasonable for loading and unloading the same and if any difference shall arise as to the reasonableness of any such charge the matter in difference shall be settled by the Board of Trade.

This Order made by the Light Railway Commissioners and modified by the Board of Trade is hereby confirmed in pursuance of Section 10 of the Light Railways Act 1896.

Given under the Seal of the Board of Trade this 2nd day of June, One thousand eight hundred and ninety-nine.

CHAS. T. RITCHIE,

President.

SEAL
OF THE
BOARD OF
TRADE.

FRANCIS J. S. HOPWOOD,

Assistant Secretary.

Left and above: Schedule of charges for non-passenger traffic on the LCBER, as appended to the 1898 Light Railway Order.

Order. This meant that the company was only now in a position to carry out its undertaking - with no time left to start, let alone finish the work!

Not until 26th September, when the Board of Trade confirmed the Llandudno and Colwyn Bay Light Railway (Deviation Amendment) Order, 1903, was the LCB&RETCo. officially granted extra time: the three-year time period for the purchase of land was increased to four years and six months and that for the completion of the works to five years, both dates to be calculated from 22nd June, 1899,

> Provided that if the actual construction of the railway of 1898 be not substantially commenced by the thirtieth day of September 1903 the powers of the Company under the Order of 1898 and this Order shall cease.

A further proviso was that Rhos Road could not be used by trams until that section of the highway occupied by the light railway had been widened, in accordance with an agreement dated 15th December, 1902 with Cayley. Presumably the work was never done as this section of the route was later altered (because of the expense involved in the widening?); it appears, though, that the land for the line between Rhos-on-Sea and the West Parade, Llandudno, was all purchased within the new time limit. The proposed route onwards from Rhos through Colwyn Bay was still not regarded as a satisfactory one and alternative plans were drawn up. As for the promise to investors included in the company's title of reaching Rhyl - indeed, it had hopes of reaching Prestatyn even further to the east - as far as is known no attempts were ever made to obtain powers for such a line and, as will be seen below, the promise quickly evaporated. Furthermore, the company was hampered by another proviso in the Order preventing it carrying out road works in Llandudno and Colwyn Bay urban districts during the months of June to September, i.e. the holiday season.

The LCB&RETCo. was now in something of a sorry state. Only 11,560 shares had been issued, of which Thomas S. Turnbull, the company's one Director, held 1,000. Of the remaining £10,560 subscribed capital, 9,530 shares were held by the Welsh Electric Traction Co. Ltd - another company with a Manchester registered office of which Morris was also the Secretary. But - in refutation of a statement made by the company's solicitor in March 1902 that 'the company had done no work, nor purchased a yard of land, and that practically all the money had been spent' - things were now about to happen.

Chapter Two

Open at Last

On 10th October, 1903 the *North Wales Chronicle* announced that work on the tramway was at long last underway: at the end of September a start had been made near Rhos on a reserved section some 1,000 yards long. A total of 33 men were engaged in filling-in and raising the route of the trackbed to the required level, erecting fences and laying sleepers. Stone for the work was obtained from a nearby quarry - nine men and eight carts were reported to be occupied in this work. From certain contemporaneous events it is clear that this move to begin construction was merely a politicial one: Llandudno UDC was again preparing to apply for a Board of Trade Order to build its own tramway in Llandudno and the town's Surveyor had already been instructed to modify the 1897 plans accordingly. Furthermore, on 26th September Cayley had written to the UDC requesting that the Council join him in petitioning the Board of Trade to stop the progress of the tramway: he claimed that the work done was not sufficient to be deemed 'a substantial commencement' under the terms of the 1903 Order. It was, in short, a very lightly-laid line to serve Mr W. Horton's brickworks!

The LCB&RETCo. continued its customary policy of uttering reassuring noises at every opportunity. W.G. Rhodes of Messrs Hewitt & Rhodes of Manchester, the engineers retained for the construction, had a meeting with the UDC and confidently stated that 'although he did not anticipate that the railway would be in full working order till Whitsuntide next', he thought that parts of it might be. Towards the end of October the Council Surveyor inspected the work done and reported that 44 men were engaged upon it and that 250 yards or so of track had been well laid - some previously condemned sleepers having been replaced!

At the beginning of November the Surveyor again visited the site and reported that the trackbed had been prepared for a distance of 800 yards, 70 men were now employed and large quantities of rails and sleepers had been delivered. Horton was now financing the work and all in all it seemed as if the tramway was fast becoming fact. By January 1904 Rhos Road had been reached and crossed for Colwyn Bay UDC received complaints about the tramway track there - the rails were supposed to lie flush with the road surface but had instead been laid 'on sleepers with shingles from the beach' heaped around them.

On 10th March, 1904 the *Tramway and Railway World* happily announced that Messrs Hewitt & Rhodes had secured the contract (which was worth £99,440) with the company - now entitled the Llandudno & Colwyn Bay Electric Traction Co. Ltd (L&CBETCo.) - for the construction of the line from Mostyn Street, Llandudno to Rhos-on-Sea. It was ready to be completed by 1st May and, according to that journal, 1½ miles had already been laid whilst work on a new contract was being commenced by sub-contractors. The truth was sadly different. At the beginning of June the company applied to the Board of Trade for another year's extension, the existing deadline expiring on the second day of that month. Track laid equalled just 365 yards.

The tramway as first laid in Gloddaeth Street, Llandudno. This view is looking towards the West Shore; here side poles gave way to span wires to support the overhead. This and the following construction photographs were captured on film for Bruce Peebles in early 1907, before the line's opening.   *Courtesy N.B. Traction Collection*

The spacious (and largely undeveloped) Gloddaeth Street again, this time looking north-east towards Hooson's Corner.   *Courtesy N.B. Traction Collection*

Lieut-Col P.G. von Donop, RE, of the Board of Trade heard the company's application for a further time extension on Friday 15th July, 1904, in the Colwyn Bay Hotel. Reporting on the meeting, the *North Wales Chronicle* of 23rd July stated that only two men (!) were engaged on building the line. According to the newspaper account, it was stated that the contract for the line had in fact been placed on 25th April with the Welsh Electric Traction Co. Ltd ('laughter'): 'The contract would be sublet for the construction because the company was not a constructing company (laughter)'. Apparently £40,000 of fresh financial backing was to be provided by a London group, the Tramways Extension Syndicate, and this induced the Board of Trade to grant a time extension until 23rd February, 1905 with the possibility of a further six months to complete and open the line if the work was progressing satisfactorily. The construction contract was due to expire on 1st May, 1905.

It must have come as no surprise to anyone when 1st May, 1905 came and went without any further work having been done on the tramway. The story now takes on a familiar ring as the promoters continued to spend what capital they could raise on raising more capital and arranging time extensions to buy more time to raise more capital to buy more time... and all the while the local councils grew more and more irate on the outside of this vicious circle. Then in 1906 the circle broke when the L&CBETCo. went into liquidation; as a stop-gap measure to salvage the company's powers a nominal company, the Caernarvonshire Electric Traction Syndicate Ltd (CETS), was formed until a new start could be made. This came on 25th July, 1906 with the registration of the Llandudno & District Electric Tramway Construction Co. Ltd (L&DETCCo.), set up to adopt agreements with the L&CBETCo. (which it absorbed on 23rd August), the CETS and the old-established (and experienced in tramway construction) Edinburgh firm of Bruce Peebles & Co. Ltd to take over the necessary powers, issue contracts for the work and equipment, complete and actually operate the line. One wonders just what the local residents expected to come of it all!

This time, however, the move was destined to suceed. The L&DETCCo. got off to a good start from the very beginning: almost all its 1,000 £100 shares were immediately issued, no doubt helped by the fact that Bruce Peebles guaranteed a 6 per cent dividend on them until 30th June, 1907. Mr A. Belton Macartney was appointed as the first company Secretary and the registered office was set up in London at 13 St Helens Place, EC; the four Directors - Stephen Sellon, MICE (Chairman), Thomas Stoker, Roland S. Portheim and R.A. Freemantle, MIEE - promptly placed the construction contract with Bruce Peebles. This Board had strong connections with other tramway and electric power companies, both at home and abroad, and as Portheim was Bruce Peebles' Managing Director it was hardly surprising that work pushed ahead on preparing the trackbed; early in 1907 tracklaying recommenced. In January two tramcars were brought to the site for trials on the line; these had originally been built for another Bruce Peebles contract (Canvey Island) but had since been returned to the manufacturer. (Further details of these cars are given in Chapter Ten.)

In startling contrast to the on-off-on efforts of the previous years, construction went forward at what must have seemed an incredible rate. It had to: the latest time extension granted was only until 21st November of that year. Under the

At Hooson's Corner, looking towards the seafront, showing the infamous passing loop right on the bend.
Courtesy N.B. Traction Collection

Looking back towards Hooson's Corner and the Great Orme from Mostyn Street, at the other end of the loop. Note the general state of the roadways in the town - something that would prove a bone of contention half a century later.
Courtesy N.B. Traction Collection

The prepared track foundations in Mostyn Broadway, looking east, with the Grand Theatre in the mid-distance and the Little Orme beyond; the then still relatively undeveloped nature of this end of the town is apparent. *Courtesy N.B. Traction Collection*

Leaving Mostyn Avenue, the tramway crossed Nant-y-Gamar Road to enter Bodafon Fields; again, looking east towards the Little Orme. *Courtesy N.B. Traction Collection*

Bodafon Fields with the track still under construction, just before it joined Bryn-y-Bia Road, looking back towards Llandudno with the sweep of Ormes Bay visible on the right.
Courtesy N.B. Traction Collection

Climbing Bryn-y-Bia Road with the overhead now supported by side poles.
Courtesy N.B. Traction Collection

The tramway's one major cutting was just over the top of Penrhyn Hill, seen here shortly after the dual overhead wires had been strung. *Courtesy N.B. Traction Collection*

Stringing the overhead wires, slightly further down Penrhyn Hill. By installing two wires at the outset, any later track-doubling would be greatly facilitated.   *Courtesy N.B. Traction Collection*

supervision of Bruce Peebles' engineer, W.C. Waite, and his assistant engineer E. Scholfield, the trackbed had been blasted out over the lower slopes of the Little Orme on its landward side (Penrhyn Hill), track laid and the overhead erected. Within a matter of months a single line of track (with passing loops being added) stretched from the newly-erected depot at Rhos-on-Sea to the West Shore, Llandudno and the full dual overhead wiring was in place. (Two wires were installed from the start to allow cars to pass with the minimum of inconvenience, and for the track on any section to be doubled at a later date without altering the overhead.) Grooved tramway rails weighing 90 lb. per yard were used throughout, spiked to wooden sleepers and ballasted on the reserved sections and laid on 18 in. wide by 9 in. deep concrete foundations on the roadway stretches, where the rails were paved with a line of wooden blocks on each side; in the centre of Llandudno these blocks were covered with tar macadam in an attempt to reduce traffic noise. (The use of tramway rails on the more rural sections, as opposed to the conventional railway rails often favoured on other similar lines, was because the company anticipated those portions of the right-of-way would soon be converted into roads; indeed, alongside parts of the line building plots were now being sold as a direct spin-off from the tramway's coming.) The overhead wires were supported by a mixture of bracket arms and span wires, with tubular poles throughout (except on some straight rural stretches where lattice-girder poles were used). Current at 500-550 volts DC was supplied by Llandudno UDC from its power station in Maesdu Road, which had opened on 5th November, 1898 equipped with an Allen steam engine and an eight-pole 300kW generator supplied by Bruce Peebles. Distribution cables were by Callender's Cable & Construction Co.

Arrangements for working the line were not neglected. A fleet of 14 single-deck cars was ordered from the Midland Railway Carriage & Wagon Co. Ltd of Shrewsbury, W.H. Moorhouse (of tramway experience at Tynemouth and Barnsley) was appointed General Manager, Sellon (formerly a member of the Board of Trade Committee on Light Railways, and Engineer to the British Electric Traction Co. Ltd) was appointed Chief Engineer, and a staff of men with at least two years' tramway experience each recruited. On Friday 9th August the first trial trips were run over the line and, according to the *Electrical Review* of the following week,

> The cars ran satisfactorily, but it is stated that the B. of T. will not grant the necessary certificate to carry passengers until the cars are provided with handbrakes in addition to the Westinghouse brakes.

This modification - if not already in hand - was soon made to the cars for on 26th September Lieut-Col von Donop inspected the completed 5 miles of line between the West Shore and the depot at Rhos-on-Sea on behalf of the Board of Trade and found them basically satisfactory; the opening was set for October. On Thursday 17th of that month the first passenger-carrying trips were made by the new cars, though the occasion was a private one for the benefit of company officials and guests; with those making the trip over the line were a party of LNWR officials, Messrs Waite and Scholfield of Bruce Peebles, and Messrs G. W. Stevenson and A.W. Thomas of the car builders.

Car No. 3 of 1907, as yet unlettered, on Penrhyn Hill during a trial run for the contractors.
Courtesy N.B. Traction Collection

No. 3 again, at the same location.   *Courtesy N.B. Traction Collection*

Marine Drive shortly after the track had been laid. Note the lattice poles on this section.
Courtesy N.B. Traction Collection

Near the site of the car shed just before its erection, with an unidentified contractor's locomotive - apparently a bodiless steam tram - at work.　　　*Courtesy N.B. Traction Collection*

The car shed with what looks like almost the entire original fleet inside, shortly after delivery - some of the car bodies are still jacked-up awaiting their trucks and wheels.

Courtesy N.B. Traction Collection

Two days later, on Saturday 19th October, 1907, the line opened to the general public with cars starting simultaneously from each end. (The first car from Llandudno is believed to have been No. 14 whilst the identity of the other has been lost.) During the afternoon and evening two more cars were brought into service to cope with the traffic. The opening was in keeping with the history of the project: no ceremony (other than cheers and bell-ringing from spectators), a limited half-hourly service and No. 11 sticking on Penryhn Hill. Nevertheless, 4,434 passenger journeys were made that day and over £45 taken in receipts. The first ticket issued was purchased by Councillor J. McMaster of Llandudno UDC Lighting Committee.

Well-loaded original car No. 14 of 1907 in a wet Mostyn Street, in what is thought to be an opening day photograph.

Author's Collection

Chapter Three

The Route Described

Finding a suitable point in the narrative at which to describe the tramway's route in detail is not an easy task for the simple reason that the details kept changing throughout the tramway's life. It will, however, be attempted here, with references included to alterations made after the line was fully open; these will also be covered in later chapters at the appropriate chronological points.

Prior to 1922 the official western end of the LCBER was situated on Llandudno's West Parade, opposite the end of Dale Street. Here, at the edge of the town, the low-lying land bordering the Conwy estuary was just beginning to be developed for housing. Two short terminal roads and a short passing loop sited some 350 yards or so from them, just before the line turned sharply right into Gloddaeth Avenue, aided car movements, otherwise this section was always single track. From 1922 onwards the official terminus was the truncated single track at the end of Gloddaeth Avenue, the 440 yards of track back round the corner and along to Dale Street being lifted that spring and the appellation 'West Shore' transferred from the old to the new terminus. In actuality, this final section had been abandoned shortly after the line opened and it was derelict by the start of World War I, a sand-swept reminder of the company's erstwhile dreams of reaching down along the coast to Deganwy.

(It should be borne in mind that in the first instance the tramway was laid throughout as a single track with passing loops added as and where it was felt they were needed. A programme of double-tracking most of the tramway was not completed until 1930, the work having been carried out in a number of stages between the opening and then. Coloured lights mounted on the traction standards controlled entry to the single line sections.)

From the West Shore the line ran straight across the Great Orme isthmus along Gloddaeth Avenue (mid-way along which was a passing loop for a while) and its extension Gloddaeth Street (another, this time long-lasting loop was sited here opposite the end of Clifton Road) before it swung abruptly right at Hooson's Corner into Mostyn Street. Somewhat bizarrely, a passing loop was laid here on the very corner - a corner that gave rise to continual complaints about the squealing of the trams as they rounded it (*see Chapter Four*). From this major crossroads in the town centre - which took its name from the large shop there, though it was also known as Palladium Corner after the threatre at the end of Gloddaeth Street - the single line ran down Mostyn Street for ¼ mile until it reached a point flanked by the Library and St John's church, where the double tracks (eventually) began.

Leaving Mostyn Street the tramway entered that road's continuation, Mostyn Broadway, passing (on the right) the North Western Hotel and (on the left) what was later to be the Crosville bus depot and the Grand Theatre. Halfway between the North Western and the Grand was a trailing crossover and in 1953 another was laid outside the theatre. Still sweeping along the main thoroughfare of Llandudno, the tramway passed on into Mostyn Avenue and

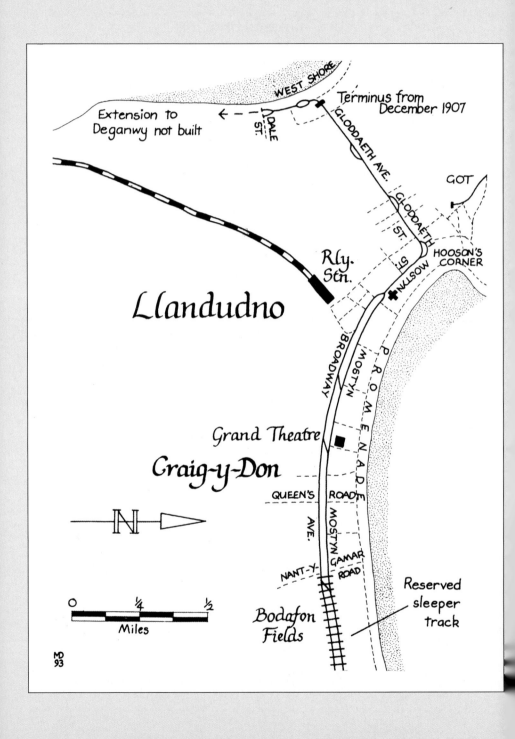

Looking up Gloddaeth Avenue, Llandudno, during the 1920s with an unidentified single-decker leaving the West Shore terminus. *Courtesy Llandudno & Colwyn Bay Tramway Society*

Gloddaeth Avenue again during the 1920s, this time looking towards the North Shore. *Courtesy Llandudno & Colwyn Bay Tramway Society*

The LCBER at the end of its life: looking from the corner of Queen's Road up an almost deserted Mostyn Broadway towards the Great Orme.   *Author's Collection*

Another postcard in the same series, this time further east, on Mostyn Avenue, on the edge of town.   *Author's Collection*

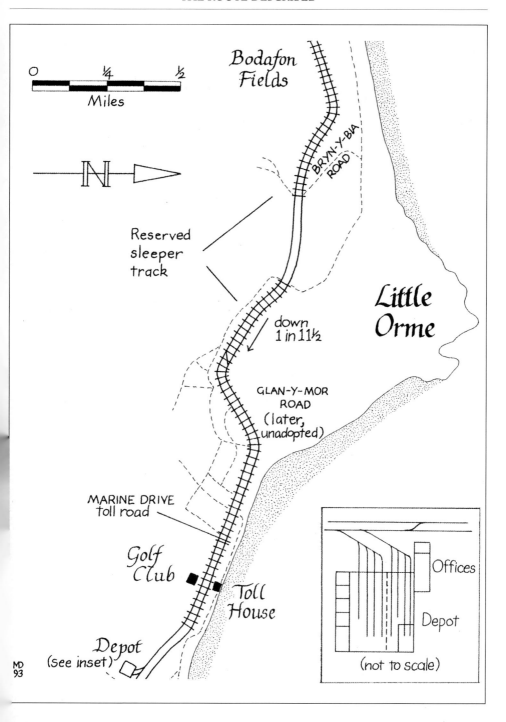

Bodafon Fields

BRYN-Y-BIA ROAD

Reserved sleeper track

down 1 in 11½

Little Orme

GLAN-Y-MOR ROAD (later, unadopted)

MARINE DRIVE toll road

Golf Club

Toll House

Depot (see inset)

Offices

Depot

(not to scale)

MD
93

O   ¼   ½
Miles

N

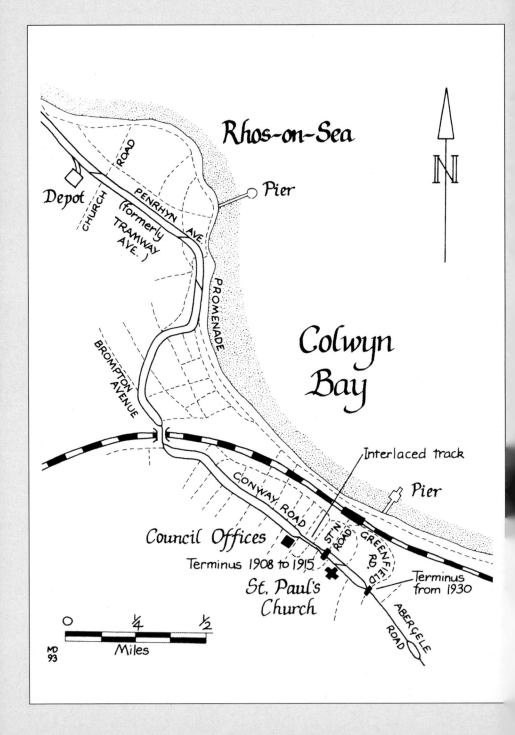

Rhos-on-Sea

Pier

Depot

CHURCH ROAD

PENRHYN AVE. (formerly TRAMWAY AVE.)

PROMENADE

BROMPTON AVENUE

Colwyn Bay

Interlaced track

Pier

CONWAY ROAD

STN. ROAD

GREENFIELD RD.

Council Offices
Terminus 1908 to 1915

St. Paul's Church

Terminus from 1930

ABERGELE ROAD

N

0   ¼   ½
Miles

MD 93

left the town centre for the outlying district of Craig-y-Don, carrying straight on over the T-junction with Nant-y-Gamar Road into its first reserved section; here there was another trailing crossover.

The line now ran through the pastoral Bodafon Fields for ¾ mile, rising ever-steeper up the lower slopes of the Little Orme above Llandudno Bay. Curving sharply right to merge with Bryn-y-Bia Road in the district known as Craigside, the tracks followed the side of the roadway for another ¼ mile to the summit of Penrhyn Hill, as this part of the Little Orme was known, just before crossing the main Llandudno-Colwyn Bay road (later the A456) on the level. Here began a 1 in 11½ descent - the line's steepest - on reserved track above and to the left of main road, the small settlement of Penryhnside on the other side of the road at the top of the hill giving its name to the tram stop here. At the bottom of Penrhyn Hill the tramway swung eastwards, still on a reserved section (which became an unadopted road and later part of Glan-y-Mor Road) and onto the open Marine Drive toll road, beside Penryhn Bay, at Orme Point. Extending between the Little Orme and Rhos-on-Sea, the bay was a trouble-prone stretch of coast along much of which the tramway occupied a company-owned toll road, some 570 yds in length, running behind the sea wall along the top of a shingle bank sandwiched between the rocky beach and Rhos Golf Club. At the far end of this section the golf clubhouse was passed on the right, and the toll-booth on the left, before the line swung inland into Rhos-on-Sea via the newly-named but unmade Tramway Avenue, reaching the depot and offices of the LCBER on the right just before another trailing crossover at the junction of the Avenue and Church Road. (Tramway Avenue was later renamed Penrhyn Avenue as the area was developed for housing.)

The tramway depot - the only one on the LCBER - was situated on the landward side of the line and was connected to the Llandudno-bound track by two trailing points; the spur from each point led to four shed roads into the depot, which (nominally) had room for 26 cars. As well as housing the trams at night, this was where all minor repairs, overhauls, repainting jobs and the like were done. Also housed here were the various staff and general offices, the latter having a frontage on the Avenue next to the depot, incorporating a waiting room for passengers as befitting its original status as the tramway's eastern terminus. (A good indication of the strong rural character of much of the line when constructed is given by the fact that this now populous district was known, when the tramway arrived, as Klondyke on account of its isolation!)

The end of Tramway Avenue was reached ½ mile beyond the depot; immediately before this a trailing crossover existed at the corner of Colwyn Crescent until 1953; this was the one relaid outside the Grand Theatre in Llandudno. The line now curved right again, in the centre of Rhos, to emerge onto Cayley Promenade, which it occupied for ¼ mile along the seafront. Then, turning inland once more, the tramway passed along Whitehall Road through the residential area on the border of Rhos and Colwyn Bay before turning into Brompton Avenue and crossing over the LNWR's main Chester-Holyhead railway line. Almost immediately beyond the road bridge it turned sharply left into Colwyn Bay's principal thoroughfare, Conway Road (later the A55 but, since its by-passing with long stretches of dual-carriageway between Abergele

Looking up Bryn-y-Bia Road on 9th June, 1938 from the top deck of a descending ex-Bournemouth car.   *D.W.K. Jones*

A misty day in November 1955 with an open-topper about to ascend Penrhyn Hill, as seen from a Colwyn Bay-bound sister car. Note the passengers' shelter at the tram stop between them.
                                                                    D.W.K. Jones

Looking towards Rhos depot during the 1920s along what is now Penrhyn Avenue, the builders' boards in the fields presaging later development. Note the lattice overhead masts used from Glan-y-Mor Road to the end of Tramway Avenue, later replaced by tubular poles (except in Glan-y-Mor Road). *Courtesy Llandudno & Colwyn Bay Tramway Society*

The undeveloped Tramway Avenue from the depot, looking towards Rhos.
Courtesy N.B. Traction Collection

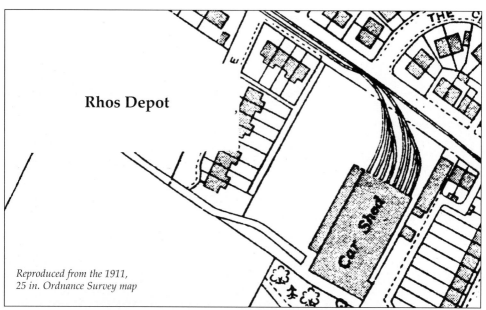

Rhos Depot

*Reproduced from the 1911,
25 in. Ordnance Survey map*

The car shed with toastracks Nos. 19 and 21, 1907 single-decker No. 18 (the renumbered 14) and No. 24 ex-Darwen. Just visible on the right is one of the ex-Bournemouth double-deckers.

D.W.K. Jones

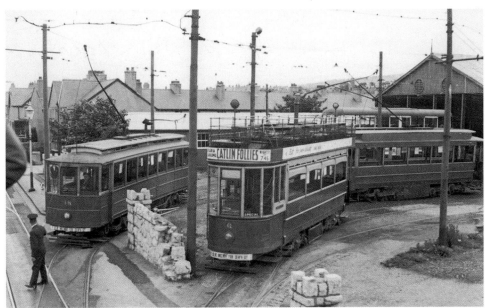

A 1951 depot line-up with (*from left to right*) No. 18 (formerly No. 14 of 1907), No. 6 (ex-Bournemouth) and one of the ex-Accrington cars, with No. 24 (ex-Darwen) behind.

D.W.K. Jones

Looking back along Tramway Avenue in the 1920s, from the cricket ground to the depot, with the Little Orme in the distance. From here to the Colwyn Bay terminus the line ran through a built-up area again. *Courtesy Llandudno & Colwyn Bay Tramway Society*

Car No. 23, on the front at Rhos-on-Sea in 1952. The pier in the distance was one dismantled in Douglas, on the Isle of Man, and re-erected here in the 1890s; it was demolished in 1954.

H.L. Runnett

Car No. 23 in Conway Road, Colwyn Bay in June 1952, bound for the terminus. On the corner of Hawarden Road is the English Presbyterian Church.   *H.L. Runnett*

Car No. 24 at Colwyn Bay in June 1952, on the local shuttle service.   *H.L. Runnett*

Toastrack No. 22 at the tramway's sometime Colwyn Bay terminus, in Abergele Road outside St Paul's church. The three footboards on this side of the car have been folded into the upright position, probably to discourage passengers from boarding from the centre of the roadway.

Author's Collection

Ex-Accrington No. 4 at the final Colwyn Bay terminus on 17th March, 1956. *Vic Bradley*

The final Colwyn Bay terminus on 20th November, 1955 with open-topper No. 8 awaiting passengers. *D.W.K. Jones*

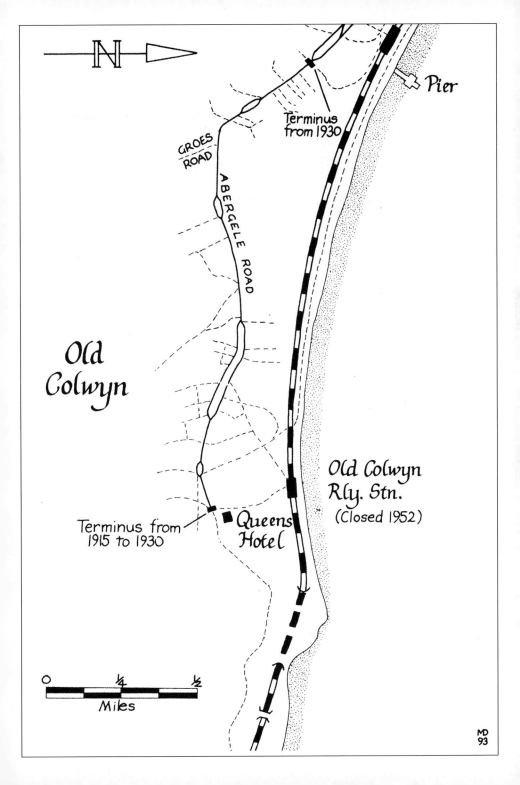

N

Pier

Terminus
from 1930

GROES
ROAD

ABERGELE ROAD

Old
Colwyn

Old Colwyn
Rly. Stn.
(Closed 1952)

Terminus from
1915 to 1930

Queens
Hotel

0   ¼   ½
Miles

MD
93

A rare view of trams on the Old Colwyn extension, with a 1907 car nearest the camera, on an undated postcard.   *Author's Collection*

and Conwy, here redesignated the A547); as the double tracks of the tramway reached the railway bridge they were briefly singled for it never proved possible to double the line over it.

For the remaining mile along Conway Road and its continuation, Abergele Road, the track was again double (though for a 200-yard stretch between the Council Offices and the top of Station Road the two tracks were interlaced on account of the narrowness of the roadway). Halfway between Station Road and the terminus, outside St Paul's church, was the line's final trailing crossover. This was not the line's final eastern terminus throughout all its life, however, for between 1915 and 1930 the tramway extended for another 1¾ miles as a single-track line, with three passing loops and a short double-track section, along Abergele Road (the old A55) into Old Colwyn, terminating by the Queens Hotel. The story of the opening and closing of this portion of the LCBER is told in the next two chapters.

Chapter Four

Expansion...

Full scheduled services over the tramway were instituted in November 1907, from Rhos Depot to the West Parade terminus in Llandudno but, as mentioned earlier, were modified the following month so that all cars terminated in Gloddaeth Avenue - 'West Shore' - instead of proceeding any further. This arrangement was stated by the company to provide a quicker service with resulting benefits to the public, and that the cars would recommence going through to Dale Street in the summer when traffic warranted it (though they never, in fact, did). Authority to construct the extension from the West Parade through the sand dunes and the golf links to Deganwy was allowed to expire, one reason being that the hoped-for housing developments along that section of coast (and hence potential traffic for the tramway) had so far failed to materialise.

In November 1906 the L&DETCCo. had applied to the Light Railway Commissioners for another Light Railway Order, partly to alter and extend the authorized route for the tramway in Colwyn Bay and partly to secure an extension of time for completion of the remainder of the authorized Colwyn Bay section of the line not yet built. This Order, confirmed by the Board of Trade on 30th September, 1907, was entitled the Llandudno and Colwyn Bay Light Railway (Extension and Amendment) Order, 1907 - a title that aptly summed up its contents. Under its provisions the route planned for Colwyn Bay by the Orders of 1898 and 1903 was abandoned in favour of 2 miles 45.52 chains of new line from the bottom of Tramway Avenue in Rhos along the Promenade, up Whitehall Road, over the Chester-Holyhead railway bridge into Conway Road and on to a point in Abergele Road 202 yards east of Groes Road. This new route was the one eventually contructed (and as described in the previous chapter), though it was in fact only about half the length the company had wanted: a 19.42-chain loop from Conway Road down Penrhyn Road towards the railway station, then back up Station Road to Abergele Road, had been included as a last attempt to reach the station but powers to construct this section of line were allowed to lapse. (The outcome was that when completed the LCBER served the two sizeable towns of its title without passing, or terminating, close to either of their railway stations, so losing out on two major sources of traffic - a most unusual situation for a British tramway.)

Time allowed for completion of the works was extended under the 1907 Order to two years from 30th September for the new lines - though construction of the last 24 chains of the extension was not permitted to commence until the company had secured powers for a full extension to Old Colwyn (*see below*). An extension of time allowance of three years (from the same date) was given for the uncompleted portion of the 1898 tramway and 12 months were allowed for the company to widen Rhos Road to 42 feet, failing which £2,500 was to be paid for the local authority to do it; a further £3,000 was to be paid directly for two widenings in Abergele Road. The Order also postponed the local authority's

Four photographs of the LCBER in its very early years, beginning with an excellent view of Mostyn Street from on high.   *G.R. Thomson Collection*

The eastern end of Bodafon Fields, with Bodafon Road in the foreground and Bryn-y-Bia Road coming in from the right.   *G.R. Thomson Collection*

A very early view of the western end of the LCBER's section by Penrhyn Bay, with holidaymakers in their Edwardian finery.   *G.R. Thomson Collection*

In Rhos, looking north from the southern end of the Promenade.   *G.R. Thomson Collection*

Pre-World War I postcard view of the then single-track tramway in Mostyn Street and Mostyn Broadway, Llandudno, with one of the 1909 single-deckers in the distance and beyond that the Great Orme. The scene is surprisingly little-changed today - except for the traffic!

Author's Collection

compulsory purchase powers until six months after 2nd June, 1941 or every subsequent seven years.

Continuing its new, dynamic policy of actually getting things done, the company immediately commenced work on the Colwyn Bay section with an Easter 1909 date set for the opening. By March of that year construction was well under way and it seemed that the deadline would be met but completion of the final touches delayed the introduction of public services, as far as the top of Station Road, until Monday 7th June. Total route mileage officially open was now 6 miles 48 chains, of which 1 mile 2 chains was double track, out of an authorized total of 8 miles 55 chains.

Now that it had at long last become a reality the tramway was handsomely meeting the expectations of its long-suffering supporters. The first General Meeting of the L&DETCCo. had been held, under the chairmanship of Sellon, on 24th March, 1908 and the receipts for 21 weeks (up to 13th March) of £1,542 announced - an average taking of over £72 per week throughout the non-tourist season; car miles were reported as 46,000 and the total number of passenger journeys 174,664. That the concern was proving a relatively prosperous one was of little doubt; 21st April, 1909 saw the company register a new, less cumbersome name: the Llandudno & Colwyn Bay Electric Railway Ltd. More tangible evidence of prosperity came later in the year when, in September, a further four single-deck cars were purchased as new (*see Chapter Ten*) from the United Electric Car Co. Ltd of Preston, bringing the stock total to an impressive eighteen. (During this year the loop referred to in Chapter Three was laid at Hooson's Corner in Llandudno as part of the provision of a better service programme.)

The fortunes of the LCBER had not escaped the notice of another company in the tramway world: Balfour, Beatty & Co. Ltd. This firm had been set up in 1909 by its joint Managing Directors, George Balfour and A.H. Beatty, to act as general and electrical engineers, contractors and operating managers for tramways, railways, lighting and power undertakings. In line with its policy of buying a sizeable interest in suitable concerns, such an interest was purchased in the LCBER Ltd and Balfour took a seat on the Board in 1910. (Apart from Balfour, Beatty & Co., he held directorships of 14 other tramway and power concerns and was a member of the council of the Tramways and Light Railways Association.)

In terms of public relations, by 1911 the honeymoon was over and the old familiar company-local authority antagonism was back again. This time it was to stay until the tramway closed nearly half a century later - and then, as will be seen, even beyond that. While the line continued to develop, in this instance by doubling its track through Rhos, compaints began to be voiced concerning the state of the track elsewhere. The Colwyn Bay Surveyor was instructed by his Council to draw up a report on the condition of the line through the town so that representations could be made to the Board of Trade; the company promised that the necessary repairs would be carried out by Easter. Complaints were also received from the public about the screeching of cars round the tight bend at Hooson's Corner; assurances were given that this would be reduced by greasing the rails. (As mentioned earlier, the problem of noise at this corner dogged the tramway throughout its life and was never really solved. At a meeting of the Llandudno UDC in March 1911 the sound was referred

Looking up Mostyn Street to Hooson's Corner, and original car No. 1, on a 1911-franked postcard. The sender has written: 'Just a line to say I have landed Llandudno. We came on 5.5 am from Preston and landed 10 am'. *Author's Collection*

Further down Mostyn Street, on a 1910-franked card. This time the sender has written: 'Just leaving here 4.45 - very nice ship' - further evidence of the part played by coastal steamers in the growth of Llandudno as a seaside resort. *Author's Collection*

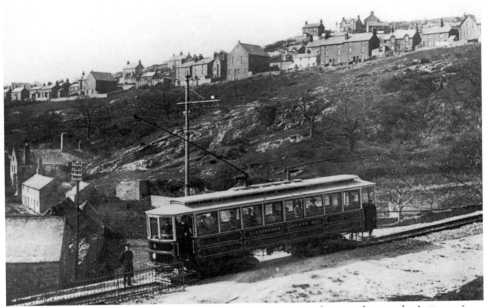

Original car No. 4 of 1907, in original livery, posed for its photograph near the bottom of Penrhyn Hill (looking towards the west).   *Oakwood Collection*

One of the tramway's original MRC&W cars entering the Promenade at Rhos, bound for Llandudno.   *Author's Collection*

A 1914-franked postcard of cars Nos. 4 and 5 of 1907 passing on Rhos (Caley) Promenade, with Colwyn Bay in the distance.   *Author's Collection*

Original car No. 12 in Colwyn Bay, loading at the 1908-1915 terminus outside the Central Hotel at the top of Station Road. The section of line behind the car is where the tracks would become interlaced during the track-doubling programme.   *Author's Collection*

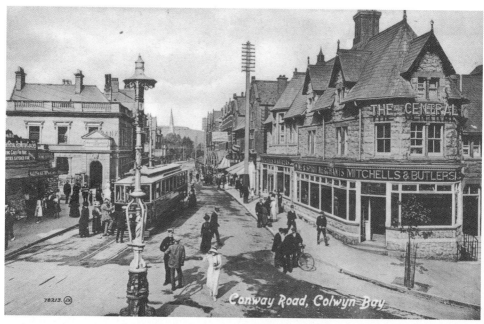

to by one member as like 'the shrieks of Kilkenny cats'.) That same year, on the evening of Thursday 22nd June, 1911 two illuminated cars were run to celebrate that day's Coronation of King George V; this was a common practice on British tramways on momentous national (or even local) occasions, a spectacular effect being achieved by swathing the designated cars in symbols, messages and other decorations made up of hundreds of electric light bulbs.

Moves to complete the extension to Old Colwyn were now coming to a head. Although the application for a Light Railway Order for this final section of line had originally been made in May 1907, in respect of a 1-mile extension along Abergele Road (estimated cost £5,870), the decision of the Light Railway Commissioners had been delayed all this time pending the outcome of a protracted dispute between the company and Colwyn Bay UDC over the road widening entailed. While the dispute dragged on a series of time extensions were successfully sought from the Board of Trade for the last section of the line authorized under the 1907 Order; these were granted in 1909, 1910 and 1911 (twice), giving a final expiration date of 30th November, 1912 for completion of the work.

In March 1911 the company put the blame for the continuing delay upon Colwyn Bay UDC, saying that an offer of £3,000 to cover the cost of the road widening had been refused, and that other obstacles had been placed in the company's way. For its part the UDC denied this and stated that the sum offered was not sufficient to cover the costs involved - and besides, it was still owed £3,000 for road widening carried out under the 1907 Order! By October the UDC was seriously considering contructing the extension itself as it regarded the terminus at the passing loop at the top of Station Road a dangerous one - especially since trams reputedly stood there illegally at night without displaying lights.

Establishments close to the route of the tramway were not loath to announce that they could be reached by the new line, as this advertisement from the *Official Guide to Llandudno* (c.1913) shows.

The matter was finally resolved by the Light Railway Commissioners with the granting of the Llandudno and Colwyn Bay Light Railway (Extension No. 2) Order, 1912, confirmed by the Board of Trade on 1st August of that year, which authorized the construction of a 1 mile 6.22-chain extension down Abergele Road from the end of the 1907-authorized line to the junction with Queen's Road. Three years were allowed for the completion of the line, during the construction of which the company was to widen Abergele Road to 24 ft wherever narrower than that (plus a footpath width of at least 6 ft).

Construction of the single-track extension was somewhat slow by the company's previous standards and the new line did not open until Friday 26th March, 1915. (The work was delayed by the track-doubling programme, which took priority; by the end of 1911 the double tracks had reached the eastern side of Penrhyn Hill on their way from Rhos to Llandudno and were within 50 yards of the loop at the summit.) Official route mileage was now 8 miles 30 chains in total, the longest of the tramway's life. Of this, 5 miles 18 chains were now double track.

With respect to other company matters, this period saw J.E. Touche and C.H. Rigg join the Board and Freemantle leave (by 1908); Bruce Peebles' Director Andrew Wilson Tate join, and Rigg and Portheim leave (by 1910); the moving of the registered office to Basildon House, Moorgate Street, London EC and the appointment (also by 1910) of A.W.R. Lovering as Secretary.

Another advertisement from the *Official Guide to Llandudno* (*c.*1913) which mentions the tramway services.

Chapter Five

...and Contraction

With the eastern end of the tramway having reached a successful conclusion, it is time to travel back to the other terminus and investigate the state of affairs there. As described in the previous chapter the original, 1898 Order authorized the line to continue on from Llandudno to Deganwy; however, the tramway as constructed, after reaching the end of Gloddaeth Avenue at the West Shore, turned expectantly southwards along West Parade only to come to an abrupt halt - like the roadway itself - some 400 yards further on opposite the end of Dale Street. Powers to construct the Deganwy extension had never been formally abandoned and time extensions had been granted along with those for the other sections of the tramway by the Board of Trade. The truth was, however, that any passenger traffic between Llandudno and Deganwy would have been a very poor second in comparison with that between Llandudno and Colwyn Bay; there was in addition a direct railway link between the two places. Capital expenditure was therefore aimed in more profitable directions and once the extension to Old Colwyn was finished the line was regarded as complete. Powers to construct the Deganwy section were accordingly permitted to elapse and when the rails to Dale Street were lifted in 1922 the LCBER's official route mileage was reduced to 8.14 miles (8 miles 10 chains). It seems that a lack of potential traffic from the few West Shore dwellings, the constant problem of wind-blown sand filling the grooves in the rails, and the fact that the beach could be accessed just as easily from the end of Gloddaeth Street, all combined to bring about this section's demise.

The following table gives some basic details of the tramway's operations during the period leading up to World War I.

Year ending 30th November	Traffic receipts £	Working expenditure £	Passengers carried	Car miles run
1907	584	2,959	63,931	13,380
1908	12,068	6,467	1,060,281	185,082
1909	14,272	10,001	1,356,323	247,843
1910	14,725	9,213	1,424,045	260,872
1911	15,359	8,001	1,505,603	267,141
1912	16,199	8,579	1,621,801	276,040
1913	17,710	8,395	1,768,142	272,908

The tramway now settled down to a fairly uneventful existence for the next dozen years or so, the first major happening of note being the purchase in 1920 of four open toastrack cars from the English Electric Co. Ltd of Preston, bringing the stock total to 22 (*see Chapter Ten*). Ordered in 1914 but with delivery delayed by the war, they were especially popular with visitors during the summer - though only when the weather was fine! - and freed-up at least some of the 1909 cars to work a shuttle service in Llandudno at busy times. The second

Toastrack No. 19 at Rhos depot as delivered in 1920, still in pieces prior to its reassembly there.
Courtesy Llandudno & Colwyn Bay Tramway Society

The trams the holidaymakers remember: toastrack No. 22 on Rhos Promenade during the 1920s.
Courtesy Llandudno & Colwyn Bay Tramway Society

The 1920s depot staff line up for the photographer against a pair of the 1909 'Yankees' ...
Courtesy Llandudno & Colwyn Bay Tramway Society

... and against the shed wall, with the edge of an inspection pit in the foreground.
Courtesy Llandudno & Colwyn Bay Tramway Society

One of only two known photographs of the 1920s trials of 1907 car No. 14 with a bow collector fitted at one end - presumably intended to eliminate de-wirements (*see also page 115*).

Courtesy Llandudno & Colwyn Bay Tramway Society

occurrence of note took place two years later when, on Saturday 18th February, 1922, the tramway's employees went on strike in protest against the company's proposal, made on 15th February, to reduce their wages by 1s. per week on top of the statutory reduction of 3s. from 1st February imposed by the National Sliding Scale. On 3rd March they agreed to a reduction of 2s. 6d. in total but did not return to work until Tuesday 4th April as, in the words of the *North Wales Weekly News* of 6th April: 'Differences afterwards arose concerning the appointment of an inspector as traffic superintendent, an appointment that was resented by the men'. Whilst the dispute continued the company took the opportunity to lift the hardly-worn rails on the abandoned West Shore section and use them to relay the ¼-mile stretch of single-track between Hooson's Corner and St John's church in Llandudno.

General improvements to the tramway were also continued throughout this period and the track-doubling programme was completed: the twin tracks now stretched from Greenfield Road, Colwyn Bay to Mostyn Street, Llandudno. The very last section of line to be so treated was the stretch in Colwyn Bay from the railway bridge to the Council Offices in Conway Road; the opportunity to carry out the work came in 1929 after the UDC had widened the road. (It should be noted in passing that as from 1st April, 1926 Colwyn Bay & Colwyn Urban District was retitled the Urban District of Colwyn Bay; on 20th September, 1934 Colwyn Bay was incorporated as a Borough and during the Charter Week celebrations one of the trams was specially decorated and, in the words of the *North Wales Pioneer* of 25th September, 'evoked well-merited praise'.)

Looking back from our modern-day vantage point it is not difficult to see that this period held the key to the future of the tramway: what took took place then was directly responsible for the eventual demise of the line a quarter of a century later, for in those inter-war years came the assertion of the motor bus for a place in the scheme of things. (To anyone acquainted with the broad outlines of British tramway history this turn of events will be a depressingly familiar one.) Motor buses had been licensed by Llandudno UDC since the early years of the 20th century, the first being operated by a firm registered in 1907 as the Llandudno Motor & Garage Co. Ltd; by World War I two more concerns, the Llandudno Coaching Co. Ltd and Messrs Jarvis & Woodyatt had joined the fray as the clamour for more licences rose.

Competition to the LCBER between Llandudno and Colwyn Bay (and even within those two towns) was inevitable. Indeed, as elsewhere in the country, it was not unknown for rival crews to come to blows over the question of 'poaching' - the bus crews' tactic of running just in front of the trams and picking up waiting passengers! In 1926 Colwyn Bay UDC (nursing memories of never having got the better of the tramway company by building the Colwyn Bay section of the line itself?) obtained powers in a general Act of Parliament to operate buses along its seafront; not to be caught on the hop the company contemplated running its own bus service there but in 1929 was forced to announce a tactical withdrawal.

In the face of both private competition and the increasing difficulties of operating through the growing holiday traffic along a narrow section of the main North Wales coast road, the decision was taken to curtail tram services at

The last section of track to be doubled (1928-9) was between the Brompton Avenue railway bridge and the 1930 terminus at Colwyn Bay , the work being carried out at the same time as the road was being widened by the UDC.   *Courtesy Llandudno & Colwyn Bay Tramway Society*

During the 1928-9 Conway Road track-doubling the two tracks between the corners of Coed Pella Road and Woodland Road were interlaced, as can be seen clearly here.
Courtesy Llandudno & Colwyn Bay Tramway Society

Another view of the track-doubling work in Conway Road, looking towards the interlaced section. *Courtesy Llandudno & Colwyn Bay Tramway Society*

More 1920s track-doubling work in progress, this time by Rhos Promenade.
Courtesy Llandudno & Colwyn Bay Tramway Society

LLANDUDNO & COLWYN BAY ELECTRIC RAILWAY LIMITED
TIME TABLE

COLWYN BAY AND LLANDUDNO—WEEK DAYS

	am	am	am	am	am	am	am	am	am	am	am	am	am	am	am			pm	pm	pm	pm	pm	pm	pm	pm	pm	pm	pm	pm	pm	pm	pm
Colwyn Bay				7 20	7 30	7 40	7 50	8 0	8 10	8 20	8 30	8 40	8 50	9 0			9 20	9 30	9 40	9 50	10 0	10 10	10 20	10 30	10 40	10 50					
Rhos-on-Sea				7 28	7 38	7 48	7 58	8 8	8 18	8 28	8 38	8 48	8 58	9 8			9 28	9 38	9 48	9 58	10 8	10 18	10 28	10 38	10 48	10 58					
Church Road	6 50	7 0	7 10	7 20	7 32	7 42	7 52	8 2	8 12	8 22	8 32	8 42	8 52	9 2			9 32	9 42	9 52	10 2	10 12	10 22	10 32	10 42	10 52	11 2					
Penrhyn Side	6 56	7 6	7 16	7 26	7 38	7 48	7 58	8 8	8 18	8 28	8 38	8 48	8 58	9 8			9 38	9 48	9 58	10 8	10 18	10 28									
Queen's Road	7 3	7 13	7 23	7 33	7 45	7 55	8 5	8 15	8 25	8 35	8 45	8 55	9 5	9 15			9 45	9 55	10 5	10 15	10 25	10 35									
Hooson's Cnr.	7 9	7 19	7 29	7 39	7 51	8 1	8 11	8 21	8 31	8 41	8 51	9 1	9 11	9 21	9 31		9 51	10 1	10 11	10 21	10 31	10 41									
Llandudno W. Shore	7 15	7 25	7 35	7 45	7 55	8 5	8 15	8 25	8 35	8 45	8 55	9 5	9 15	9 25	9 35		9 55	10 5	10 15	10 25	10 35	10 45									

(Then every 10 minutes until)

LLANDUDNO AND COLWYN BAY—WEEK DAYS

	am	am	am	am	am	am	am	am	am	am	am	am	am	am			pm	pm	pm	pm	pm	pm	pm	pm	pm	pm	pm	pm
Llandudno W. Shore				7 15	7 25	7 35	7 45	7 55	8 5	8 15	8 25	8 35	8 45	8 55	9 5		9 15	9 25	9 35	9 45	9 55	10 5	10 15	10 25	10 35	10 50		
Hooson's Cnr.				7 19	7 29	7 39	7 49	7 59	8 9	8 19	8 29	8 39	8 49	8 59	9 9		9 19	9 29	9 39	9 49	9 59	10 9	10 19	10 29	10 39	10 54		
Queen's Road				7 25	7 35	7 45	7 55	8 5	8 15	8 25	8 35	8 45	8 55	9 5	9 15		9 25	9 35	9 45	9 55	10 5	10 15	10 25	10 35	10 45	11 0		
Penrhyn Side				7 32	7 42	7 52	8 2	8 12	8 22	8 32	8 42	8 52	9 2	9 12	9 22		9 32	9 42	9 52	10 2	10 12	10 22	10 32	10 42	10 52	11 7		
Church Road	7 5	7 15	7 25	7 37	7 47	7 57	8 7	8 17	8 27	8 37	8 47	8 57	9 7	9 17	9 27		9 37	9 47	9 57	10 7	10 17	10 27	10 37	10 47	10 57	11 12		
Rhos-on-Sea	7 9	7 19	7 29	7 42	7 52	8 2	8 12	8 22	8 32	8 42	8 52	9 2	9 12	9 22	9 32		9 42	9 52	10 2	10 12	10 22	10 32	10 42					
Colwyn Bay	7 20	7 30	7 40	7 50	8 0	8 10	8 20	8 30	8 40	8 50	9 0	9 10	9 20	9 30	9 40		9 50	10 0	10 10	10 20	10 30	10 40	10 50					

(Then every 10 minutes until)

Augmented at Week-ends and Holiday Periods.

* Subject to slight alteration to meet the requirements of Llandudno Theatres.

† These cars connect with the Club Train at Colwyn Bay.

COLWYN BAY AND LLANDUDNO—SUNDAYS

	pm	pm	pm	pm	pm	pm	pm	pm			pm	pm	pm	pm	pm	pm	pm	pm	pm	pm
Colwyn Bay		12 15		12 46		1 16	1 32	1 48	2 4			8 12	8 28	8 44	9 0	9 16	9 32	9 48	10 4	10 20	10 36	10 50
Rhos-on-Sea		12 25		12 54		1 24	1 42	1 58	2 14			8 20	8 38	8 54	9 10	9 26	9 42	9 58	10 14	10 30	10 46	11 0
Penrhyn Side	11 53	12 35	12 48	1 4	1 20	1 36	1 52	2 8	2 24			8 32	8 48	9 4	9 20	9 36	9 52	10 8			
Queen's Road	12 0	12 41	12 55	1 11	1 26	1 42	1 58	2 14	2 30			8 38	8 54	9 10	9 26	9 42	9 58	10 14			
Hooson's Cnr.	12 5	12 47	1 1	1 17	1 32	1 48	2 4	2 20	2 36			8 44	9 0	9 16	9 32	9 48	10 4	10 20			
Llandudno W. Shore	12 9	12 51	1 5	1 21	1 36	1 52	2 8	2 24	2 40			8 48	9 4	9 20	9 36	9 52	10 8	10 24			

(Then every 16 minutes until)

LLANDUDNO AND COLWYN BAY—SUNDAYS

	pm	pm	pm	pm	pm	pm	pm	pm			pm	pm	pm	pm	pm	pm	pm	pm	pm	pm
Llandudno W. Shore		12 10	12 52	1 6	1 22	1 38	1 54	2 10			8 18	8 34	8 50	9 6	9 22	9 38	9 54	10 10	10 26	
Hooson's Cnr.		12 14	12 56	1 12	1 28	1 44	2 0	2 16			8 24	8 40	8 56	9 12	9 28	9 44	10 0	10 16	10 32	
Queen's Road		12 20	1 2	1 18	1 34	1 50	2 6	2 22			8 30	8 46	9 2	9 18	9 34	9 50	10 6	10 22	10 38	
Penrhyn Side		12 28	1 10	1 26	1 42	1 58	2 14	2 30			8 38	8 54	9 10	9 26	9 42	9 58	10 14	10 30	10 46	
Rhos-on-Sea	12 5	12 36	1 5	1 20	1 36	1 52	2 8	2 24	2 40			8 48	9 4	9 20	9 36	9 52	10 8	10 14	10 40	10 56
Colwyn Bay	12 15	12 45	1 15	1 30	1 46	2 2	2 18	2 34	2 50			8 58	9 14	9 30	9 46	10 2	10 18	10 34	10 50	

(Then every 16 minutes until)

The Company will endeavour to conform to the above Time Table, but will not hold themselves responsible for any delay or **inconvenience** caused by unforseen circumstances.

April, 1933.

W. G. HAMILTON, A.M.I.E.E., General Manager.

Printed by Leigh & Williams, Ltd. Colwyn Bay.

LCBER spring timetable for 1933.

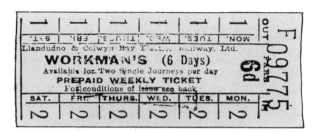

LCBER 1933 concessionary fares table and workmen's *6d.* weekly return ticket (grey).

LLANDUDNO & COLWYN BAY ELECTRIC RLY. LTD.

Workmen's Weekly Tickets and Scholar's 5 & 6-Day Weekly Tickets

The above are issued by conductors and can also be purchased at the Car Depot, Rhos-on-Sea, in accordance with the scale of charges set out below.

Where the ordinary single Fares are	Workmen's Weekly are		Scholar's Weekly are	
			6 Days	5 Days
	s. d.		s. d.	s. d.
1d.	6	...	6°	...
2d.	1 0	...	9°	...
3d.	1 6	...	1 3°	...
4d.	2 0	...	1 6°	... 1 3°
5d.	2 6	...	2 0°	... 1 8°
6d.	3 0	...	2 3°	... 1 10½°
7d.	3 6	...	2 9°	... 2 3°
8d.	4 0	...	3 0	... 2 6

Workmen's and Scholar's Weekly Tickets are available for one outward and return journey each day, except those marked thus ° which are available for two journeys per day, both outward and return.

Workmen's Weekly Tickets are only available before 9 a.m. for the outward journey.

Tramway Depot,
  Rhos-on-Sea.

W. G. HAMILTON, A.M.I.E.E.,

February, 1933.

General Manager.

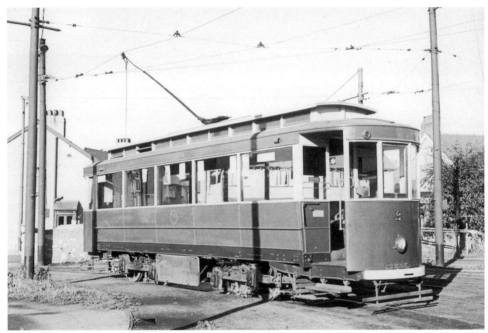

Ex-Accrington car No. 2 in 1938, at the entrance to the depot yard.   *D.W.K. Jones*

Ex-Accrington No. 5 outside the depot on 9th June, 1938.   *D.W.K. Jones*

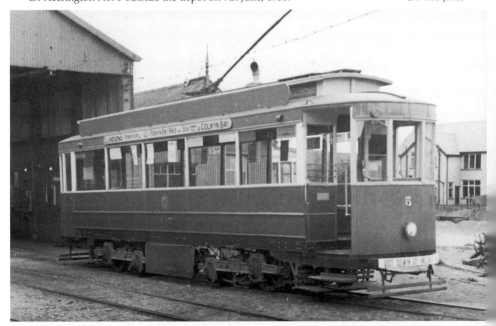

the end of the double-track section at the Greenfield Road-Abergele Road junction in Colwyn Bay; operationally, matters had not been helped by the single-track, dead-end nature of this portion of the tramway - it was not unknown for cars travelling in opposite directions to meet there head-on! - and during mornings at least often only alternate scheduled cars worked over it. As from Monday 22nd September, 1930 the single-track section from here to Old Colwyn was abandoned and Crosville Motor Services Ltd - by far the largest bus-operator across the whole of North Wales - stepped in smartly to fill the gap; the tramway company did, however, have the foresight to obtain a licence to run buses over the rest of the route if ever the tramway was forced to close.

The LCBER now consisted, in its final form, of 5.72 miles of double and 0.82 miles of single track, totalling 6.54 route miles in all. (After the closure of the Old Colwyn section, all services terminated outside St Paul's church in Colwyn Bay for some weeks until the north side of the roadway at the new terminus by Greenfield Road had been widened sufficiently to enable traffic to pass either side of a tramcar standing on the short terminal stub in the middle of the road. Not long after this, though, St Paul's became the terminus again for several years as a result of a dispute over fares - *see Chapter Nine*.)

At the start of the 1930s the company's Directors were Balfour, Lovering, Williams and a new Chairman, Col Sir Joseph Nall, DSO; by this date Lovering was also a Delhi tramway and Barbados electricity Director whilst Nall was on the Boards of several bus and tramway companies - the latter including those of Leamington & Warwick, Cheltenham, Mansfield and Nottinghamshire & Derbyshire (the last three as Chairman) - as well as running the large road haulage family business of Joseph Nall & Co. Ltd based in Manchester. By the end of 1937 both Williams and Balfour had left, replaced by R.E. Birch.

Crosville was at this time busy strengthening its hold upon the bus services of the area: on 1st May, 1930 it took over Brookes Bros of Rhyl, on 1st August North Wales Silver Motors Ltd of Llandudno and, on 18th February of the following year, the Llandudno Coaching & Carriage Co. Ltd. It must now have started to become clear that the trams, as elsewhere in many towns and cities across Britain, would sooner or later be displaced by buses as patterns of private and public transport - and, crucially, the attitude of many local authorities towards tramways - changed. The fact that it was later rather than sooner was simply due to the cost involved in resurfacing the roadway after the removal of the tracks; this same obstacle effectively put paid to the company's 1931 proposal to replace the trams with trolleybuses, as was then current Balfour, Beatty policy (so retaining use of the overhead equipment). It was decided instead to continue with the trams, replacing most of the existing ailing stock with more modern second-hand cars from other systems. Accordingly in 1932 and 1933 five single-deckers were purchased from Accrington Corporation (whose tramways had shut down early in 1932) and in 1936 ten open-top double-deckers were bought from Bournemouth (another system closure). Although these were the LCBER's first double-deckers, Board of Trade permission to run such cars between Old Colwyn and Penrhyn Bay had been providently obtained as long ago as 1916; this permission was now extended to the whole system, providing no passengers were carried on the upper decks on

Toastrack No. 19 climbs the Little Orme, in the summer of 1938, with a full complement of passengers in the care of the immaculately-clad crew. The driver is Colin Forbes. *D.W.K. Jones*

Car No. 1 (ex-Accrington) starting off from the West Shore on 9th June, 1938.   *D.W.K. Jones*

the exposed stretch of the line at Penrhyn Bay and up over the Little Orme when the wind speed exceeded 50 mph. (A wind-gauge mounted on a pole by the toll-booth originally provided the neccessary warning but when this fell into disuse near the end of the tramway's life the double-deckers were simply taken out of service when high winds seemed likely.)

On the face of it the tramway appeared to be enjoying a period of reasonable prosperity: it had a new Manager (W.G. Hamilton, AMIEE of Bournemouth, from 1931), a second source of power (a new sub-station in Ivy Road, Colwyn Bay opened in 1932 and current for the eastern section of the line was now taken from there), new wiring (in 1938 the entire overhead was renewed) and a fleet of 'new' cars. The real truth was rather different: an important section of line had had to be abandoned, the only replacement cars that could be afforded were at least 10 years old, and the company was after all in the public transport, rather than exclusively tramway, business. When all was said and done, it was only the cost of its abandonment that was keeping the line open. The special circumstances of the war years about to come would only ward off the inevitable for a little while longer.

The following table gives some basic details of the tramway's operations during World War I and the inter-war period.

Year ending 31st December	Traffic receipts £	Working expenditure £	Passengers carried	Car miles run
1914*	15,672	8,404	1,663,887	273,467
1915*	17,482	9,219	2,061,106	288,152
1916*	18,773	10,167	2,128,680	301,603
1917*	18,061	10,011	2,050,089	267,449
1918*	23,249	12,160	2,329,358	252,080
1919*	30,633	24,270	2,879,636	282,070
1920*	34,024	26,308	2,903,646	292,380
1921*	38,035	27,417	2,327,337	264,164
1922*	34,577	25,164	2,231,983	306,871
1923*	35,351	27,354	2,444,170	361,588
1924*	29,916	26,822	2,193,579	372,935
1925*	28,029	23,450	2,353,966	410,803
1926†	26,704	26,697	2,446,228	462,516
1927	22,505	21,662	2,049,657	428,353
1928	20,663	20,980	2,250,829	442,910
1929	20,910	20,773	2,436,826	464,472
1930	15,830	18,161	1,993,640	387,392
1931	14,635	14,840	1,779,505	406,533
1932	17,415	15,899	2,119,262	487,843
1933	19,700	16,718	2,399,831	437,698
1934	19,948	16,353	2,519,192	424,478
1935	19,341	17,446	2,485,782	428,207
1936	18,943	16,702	2,541,569	423,459
1937	20,086	16,152	2,625,259	417,992
1938	19,392	16,202	2,574,205	420,500
1939	20,056	16,286	2,657,586	405,793

* year ending 30th November
† 13 months ending 31st December

One of the 1909 cars - possibly No. 18 - in Rhos depot yard, photographed from the top of a double-deck tram in August 1939 and still looking fairly intact three years after it was officially withdrawn.   *Peter Johnson Collection*

Car No. 7 at the West Shore terminus on 27th October, 1940, in wartime guise.
                                                                                    Peter Johnson Collection

Chapter Six

World War II and After

Throughout the duration of World War II the tramway continued its uninterrupted run of daily operation. To the general public, the most obvious consequences of hostilities with regard to the trams were the blacking-out of their windows at night and the use of blue bulbs for internal lighting in accordance with the blackout regulations; the car headlamps were also masked, replaced by small Board of Trade-issue lamps hung in the front and rear windows (the rear one having removeable red glass slotted over the lens). The only inconvenience occasioned seems to have been that whenever the air raid sirens were sounded at night as German planes flew along the coast to bomb Liverpool, the trams stopped running so that flashes from the overhead would not be seen by the bombers' crews and used as a navigation aid. Indirectly the war had many effects upon the tramway, the principal one being a welcome increase in passenger figures caused by an influx of a great many Government officers and service personnel into the area. A further bounty came in the shape of car drivers forced to desert their vehicles in favour of the tramway, victims of petrol rationing (with Crosville likewise benefitting). Another result of the rationing was the introduction of various special services, one of which was a 'staff car' for employees returning home after evening duties; another was an extra shuttle service (the 'Llandudno Local') between the West Shore and Craig-y-Don, whilst still another was the hiring-out of tramcars on Sundays for private excursions. The last major change occasioned by the war was one repeated on virtually all other tramway systems in Britain: the employment of conductresses, a consequence of able-bodied men being conscripted into the armed forces.

Although never on the receiving end of any war damage, three incidents did occur on the tramway at this time which need mentioning. The first took place in the spring of 1943 when gales and heavy seas caused the collapse of what passed for a sea wall beside the toll road along Penrhyn Bay; several tons of debris were deposited on the line and the golf course was flooded. Similar, though less damaging, events had occurred in 1927 and 1933 and in October 1945 exactly the same thing happened again, only this time with more serious results: the tramway formation was so undermined that the seaward track of the two was declared unsafe and for two weeks, whilst the damage was repaired, single-line working was in force over the inner track between the crossovers at Penrhyn Hill and the depot. The third and final incident took place in November 1945 when car No. 16 (originally car 6 of 1907) ran a hot axlebox, caught fire and had to be scrapped. (The cause was almost certainly insufficient lubrication, levels and standards of car maintenance being common tramway casualties of the war as a result of drastically-reduced staff numbers.)

The company emerged from the war years in optimistic mood, promptly ordering in January 1946 two second-hand double-deck cars, at a cost of £400 each, from Darwen Corporation in Lancashire (which system was about to close). These were of a far more modern design than anything possessed by the

No. 1 (ex-Accrington), in its new green and cream livery, about to make a run at the 1 in 11½ ascent of Penrhyn Hill during World War II - note the masked headlamp and its Board of Trade replacement in the front window on the left.   *D.W.K. Jones*

Car No. 3, ex-Accrington, about to leave the reserved section at the top of Penrhyn Hill, during World War II - note again the masked headlamp on the tram - with the shape of things to come represented by the Crosville Leyland bus on the right.   *D.W.K. Jones*

General view of the depot at 3.40 pm on Wednesday 29th May, 1946. *Left to right*: Nos. 17, second-hand 13, works car 23, and second-hand 11, 1 and 10. *E.N.C. Haywood*

Original car No. 17 (renumbered from 11) at Hooson's Corner on 19th June, 1945.
E.N.C. Haywood

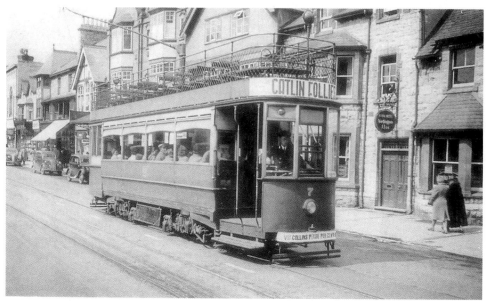

Car No. 7 in Abergele Road, Colwyn Bay - the last stop before the terminus - on 28th May, 1946.
E.N.C. Haywood

Open-topper No. 11 having to work 'wrong line' from Glan-y-Mor Road after the track at
Penrhyn Bay suffered damage during the 1948/9 winter.   *D.W.K. Jones*

LCBER - they dated from just before the war - and were allocated new numbers 23 and 24; they were to be the last items of rolling stock to come to the line. After regauging from 4 ft, trials, driver training and so forth, a Ministry of Transport test was held on the cars on 14th April, 1948 with an outcome that came as both a shock and a disappointment to the company: on account of their high-sided, closed bodywork the new cars would not be permitted to operate in public service, at any time, on the section through Bodafon Fields, over Penrhyn Hill, along the coastal stretch and on to the depot because of the danger of their turning over in windy conditions. Consequently No. 23 entered service on Thursday 22nd April on the 'Llandudno Local' between Nant-y-Gamar Road and the West Shore, followed by No. 24 on a similar shuttle service between the depot and the Colwyn Bay terminus.

Meanwhile the never-ending task of maintaining the permanent way to the required standard continued: the first major section to be tackled after the war was that in Penrhyn Avenue from the depot to Colwyn Crescent. One track at a time was relaid - resulting in single-line working throughout 1946 and 1947 - though for some reason one track was laid on a new concrete bed and the other on ballasted sleepers, both then being metalled over; presumably this was done to facilitate any possible future singling of the line.

Elsewhere on the tramway, the stretch along Penrhyn Bay was by now a notorious trouble-spot and during the winter of 1948/9 the line was once again damaged by heavy seas and the ground under the seaward track was washed away. Again it was necessary to put single-line working into operation while the formation was repaired, this time aided by new crossovers laid at Maesgwyn Road and the golf clubhouse either side of the affected section so as to reduce disruption of normal services to a minimum. Four winters later, in 1952/3, the very same thing happened yet again. This time, an attempt was made to reinforce the sea defences by hauling boulders up the beach using a winch attached to car No. 17 but was abandoned as too difficult and too costly. Consequently, thereafter only the westbound track was used between the two crossovers, with the two overhead wires restrung close together over it using replacement traction standards and bracket arms acquired from Stockport Corporation in 1951 as spares. The outer track was left to disappear under piles of shingle, and later suffer piecemeal obliteration in the construction of a new sea wall.

The ex-Stockport poles were not the only second-hand items to be purchased for the tramway as future replacements for aged and failing equipment. (The post-World War II years saw a bustle of activity in the British tramway second-hand market, with the handful of surviving lines able to pick over the remains of their closing counterparts.) In November 1952 more tubular standards, a number of steel wheel tyres and several items of depot equipment were bought from Birmingham Corporation; the following year a number of Dick, Kerr type '30B' motors, gears, axles and wheels, and a quantity of seat cushions were obtained from the same source, while in 1954 four sets of Dick, Kerr type 'K4' controllers were acquired from Sunderland Corporation. These spares were made available by the closures of the Birmingham system in 1953 and Sunderland in 1954 - both ominous omens for the LCBER. (See Chapter Ten for details of the subsequent modifications made to the LCBER cars.)

Original 1907 car No. 18 (formerly 14) outside the depot in 1949, with second-hand acquisitions No. 3 (ex-Accrington) on the right and No. 24 (ex-Darwen) inside the shed.   *D.W.K. Jones*

Open-topper No. 9 leaving the reserved Bodafon Fields section to cross Nant-y-Gamar Road shortly after World War II. A typical tiny LCBER shelter for passengers is on the right.

D.W.K. Jones

Open-topper No. 13, in service, being passed by the 1951 Light Railway Transport League
special at the crossover outside the Little Orme Café in Glan-y-Mor Road. *D.W.K. Jones*

A cold, damp day in March 1951 with open-topper No. 15 and (renumbered) No. 18 of 1907
passing at Hooson's Corner. *Peter Johnson Collection*

A busy moment at Hooson's Corner with Nos. 2 and 5 (both ex-Accrington) being passed by open-topper No. 15.   *D.W.K. Jones*

No. 24 outside the depot on 21st May, 1951.   *D.W.K. Jones*

Several minor track alterations also took place during the early 1950s. In November 1952 the single-track section in Mostyn Street was lifted and relaid, and whilst this work was in progress cars for Colwyn Bay started from Mostyn Broadway (with the West Shore being served by a shuttle from round the corner in Gloddaeth Street). The autumn of 1953 saw the re-sleepering of the reserved section between Nant-y-Gamar Road and Penrhyn Hill, the transfer of the trailing crossover from the Colwyn Crescent end of Penrhyn Avenue to Mostyn Broadway, and the laying of a sewer under the Rhos end of the toll road. (While this last task was carried out passengers and crews walked over the break to change cars.) The moving of the crossover was done to help deal with a welcome increase in traffic: cars from Colwyn Bay could now terminate in Mostyn Broadway by the Grand and Arcadia theatres, and pick up the queuing crowds waiting to go back on them. Following complaints from the Council in 1953 over the state of the track and roadways in Llandudno, the company gave an assurance that future repairs would be more substantial; in 1954 sections of track in Mostyn Broadway were accordingly relaid and re-tarred.

To return to the problem of Penrhyn Bay: in the summer of 1953 the local authorities concerned were given a government grant to construct a new set of sea defences (including the new sea wall mentioned above). The work was carried out during 1953, resulting in the permanent singling of the tramway there; after its completion a public inquiry was held at the beginning of 1954 to hear objections from the LCBER and local residents. The latter claimed that the cost of the work had been excessive and for the money spent a promenade could easily have been incorporated into the new structure; the company on the other hand claimed that it was the authorities' intention to construct a new coast road along the sea wall, thus depriving it of its tolls it collected on the existing roadway. In reply the authorities denied any intent to construct a new road - but admitted that the work done would facilitate the construction of a coast road at a later date! All of which added fuel to the company's growing belief that Llandudno UDC was anxious to see the back of the trams, hence its constant complaints about the state of the track and the roads. (It should be mentioned that the Council's complaints were not without foundation: judging by the accounts of those who can recall seeing them, the corrugations on the surfaces of the rails at Penrhyn Bay were probably the largest ever seen on a British tramway!)

The Council was not the only body that would profit by the closure of the tramway. The Chairman of the LCBER, Sir Joseph Nall, announced traffic figures for 1953 as follows:

Passengers:	2,744,593
Receipts:	£31,137
Loss:	£1,222

One hopes that Sir Joseph - to give him his full title, Colonel Sir Joseph Nall, DSO, TD, DL, JP, M Inst T - gained some small measure of satisfaction from his being created a baronet in the coming New Year's Honours List, for on 10th November, 1954 at the company's annual general meeting in London, he announced even worse figures for that year:

No. 23 (ex-Darwen), at the LCBER's final Colwyn Bay terminus, working the shuttle service from Rhos.   *Author's Collection*

Car No. 24 on the interlaced track in Colwyn Bay, May 1951. The destination blinds read 'Private Car'.   *D.W.K. Jones*

Car No. 24 and its crew outside Rhos depot in 1952. Only six LCBER staff were qualified to drive this vehicle and sister car No. 23 on account of their Westinghouse air brakes and unusual controllers.

H.L. Runnett

Toastrack No. 20 with a full load leaving the Penrhyn Hill reserved section to enter Bryn-y-Bia Road in August 1955. Note the conductor collecting fares from the footboard.

John Edgington

Passengers:	2,697,994
Receipts:	£30,906
Loss:	£3,004

In the light of the financial state of the company the Directors were seriously contemplating replacing the trams with motor buses. As the Chairman's statement to shareholders put it:

> The Directors have for some time been considering the advisability of substituting motor buses in place of trams, and as a first step towards this, application is being made to the Licensing Authority for the granting of a road service licence. It is considered that the operation of motor buses, although not possessing the present-day novelty of trams, would be more attractive to the travelling public and of benefit to the company.

The company now had four Directors, Messrs Nall, Lovering and Birch having been joined by Stanley Dudman, M Inst T in 1946; four years later the registered office had moved to Suffolk House, Laurence Pountney Hill, Cannon Street, London EC4. Birch left the Board in 1952, and Lovering the following year; their replacement appointees were J.R. Amphlett as a Director and D.R.P. Baker as company Secretary.

Appeals against the decision, and proposals by tramway enthusiasts that a preservation body of volunteers should step in to operate it - an almost unheard-of idea recently pioneered on the Talyllyn Railway in mid-Wales - or that Llandudno UDC should purchase the line and run it summer seasons only in much the same way as it operated the Great Orme line, which it had purchased at the end of 1948, were made in a valiant but (as it soon became plain) futile effort to save from closure the last 3 ft 6 in. gauge electric tramway - and the last privately-owned tramway - in the country.

Second-hand cars 1 and 14 passing in Mostyn Street, Llandudno in August 1955, both laden with holidaymakers. *John Edgington*

Mostyn Street on 11th August, 1955 with open-topper No. 9 trundling along.   *John Edgington*

Viewed from a waiting toastrack car, open-topper No. 10 leaves the single-track section at Penrhyn Bay by the golf clubhouse on 11th August, 1955.   *John Edgington*

Chapter Seven

Closure

On Wednesday 14th September, 1955 came the long-expected announcement: despite the Directors' recognition of the 'novelty of trams' (and what would that novelty be worth to Llandudno today?) the tramway was definitely to close before the year was out, and to add weight to the decision a second-hand bus was purchased from the East Kent Road Car Co. Ltd for the purpose of (re)training drivers. Circumstances, however, dictated otherwise and it became apparent that the trams would, after all, see in the New Year. The first delay was made evident on 12th October when the Chairman of the North Western Area Traffic Commissioners declared that the LCBER would have to agree to a joint bus timetable with Crosville, and then have it approved by the Commissioners, before the company's bus service could begin.

A second delay came on 1st November when a meeting was held in Colwyn Bay to decide the future of the tracks and roads used by the tramway, with representatives of the company, the local authorities and the Ministry of Transport all present. The outcome of the meeting was that no agreement could as yet be reached as to who was responsible for making good the roadways after the rails were lifted, though the local authorities remained unmoved from their conviction that, under the original 1898 Light Railway Order, the onus rested fairly and squarely upon the tramway company. The company, of course, disagreed.

At the same time it had become imperative from the company's point of view that tramway operations ceased before the summer of 1956. The reason for this was a simple financial one: the company's contract for the supply of current for the overhead with the Merseyside & North Wales Electricity Board (MANWEB) - which in 1947 had acquired the municipal power stations of both Llandudno and Colwyn Bay - was due to expire then. MANWEB presented the company with a choice of two alternative future courses of action: pay a new charge of £100 a day for the supply or else take over the relevant - and otherwise obsolete - DC generating plant from them and install it behind the depot. (It should be noted that MANWEB employed eight full-time men, plus four relief staff, to operate this plant at its sub-stations in Colwyn Bay and Cwm Road, Llandudno.) Neither of these alternatives was within the existing financial means of the company and a closure date of Saturday 24th March, 1956 was promptly announced, it being a case of cutting further losses as quickly as possible, then settling the thorny question of track removal. Eight cars were allocated to work what services would be operated in 1956: three of the ex-Accrington single-deckers and five of the ex-Bournemouth double-deckers. The remainder of the fleet was ear-marked for withdrawal as soon as any maintenance work became necessary, with four of the first cars to go being Nos. 1 and 2 (ex-Accrington) and Nos. 9 and 10 (ex-Bournemouth), scrapped that January.

And so the cold, grey, appointed day of closure arrived. Not surprisingly, the tramcars were packed to capacity all that day with local residents, tramway

Open-topper No. 11 in Glan-y-Mor Road on 7th September, 1955, having just descended Penrhyn Hill.   *Peter Johnson Collection*

Stopped in the deserted road by the Little Orme Café in Penrhyn Bay on 7th September, 1955, open-topper No. 8 takes on some additional passengers.   *Peter Johnson Collection*

No. 20 getting ready to depart from Llandudno's West Shore terminus on 7th September, 1955.
Note the sticker for Llandudno Pier - a short walk away from Hooson's Corner.
Peter Johnson Collection

A timeless view of Bodafon Fields with two open-toppers about to pass. The Little Orme is in
the distance.   *D.W.K. Jones*

Car No. 1 (ex- Accrington) at the West Shore on 11th August, 1955.   *John Edgington*

Open-topper No. 7 in Colwyn Bay on 21st November, 1955, about to leave the interlaced section of track in Conway Road.   *D.W.K. Jones*

A crowded depot in November 1955 with three toastracks, original No. 17 (ex-11), second-hand Nos. 2 and 4 (ex-Accrington), one of the ex-Darwen cars and a tower wagon all managing to squeeze into the picture. *D.W.K. Jones*

The crew of open-topper No. 8 enjoy a brief stop-over at the West Shore in November 1955; the driver is Reg Johnson. Note the conductor's heavy clothing - essential on the top deck in a Welsh winter. *D.W.K. Jones*

Sad scenes at Rhos depot as car-scrapping gets underway: outside...   *D.W.K. Jones*

...and inside.   *D.W.K. Jones*

Two more depot scenes during the LCBER's final days. An enthusiasts' special prepares to depart ...
D.W.K. Jones

...and a packed car shed.
D.W.K. Jones

Two post-World War II views inside Rhos depot. Here original survivor No. 18 (renumbered from 14) lines up with one of the ex-Darwen double-deckers...   *D.W.K. Jones*

...whilst both ex-Darwen cars are seen here in the company of toastrack No. 21.   *D.W.K. Jones*

enthusiasts and other visitors - including a party of former Bournemouth tram drivers who had a chance to try their hands again at the controls of one of their old charges - No. 8. As the winter timetable was still in operation, only four cars (single- and double-deckers) were officially in service, but one of the open-toppers (No. 11) suffered a broken lifeguard in the afternoon and another (No. 13) was substituted for it, which meant - counting No. 8 - that six cars were run over the tramway that day. At the depot, the doors were metaphorically thrown open, with enthusiasts and residents alike given the opportunity to inspect the shed and cars - and the chance to purchase whatever items they liked as souvenirs.

The official part of the proceedings began with an evening cocktail party at the Imperial Hotel in Llandudno, hosted by the company's Deputy Chairman, Stanley Dudman. Meanwhile the official 'Last Car', No. 8, was brought up from the depot under the guidance of driver 'Farmer' Dick Hughes and conductor Bob Morgan - long-standing employees of 39 and 37 years' service respectively. At 10.20 pm the official party, made up of representatives of the company , the local authorities, the police and Crosville Motor Services - totalling a hundred or so in all - clambered aboard No. 8 outside the North Western Hotel on Mostyn Broadway. With chief inspector J. Ernie Woolley at the controls, and watched by a large crowd of onlookers and well-wishers, the loaded tram moved off towards the West Shore terminus, closely followed by ex-Accrington No. 4, in the care of Percy Larkman, which was carrying the LCBER's last fare-paying passengers.

Open-topper No. 11 awaiting passengers at the West Shore terminus, 17th March, 1956; behind the houses can be glimpsed the distinctive southern slopes of the Great Orme.
Vic Bradley

Rhos depot on the last day of public service with No. 24, No. 5 (ex-Accrington), No. 13 (ex-Bournemouth) and toastrack No. 20 on show.   *Vic Bradley*

Open-topper No. 11 undergoing running repairs outside the depot on the very last day of public service. On the right is the shape of things to come on the morrow.   *Vic Bradley*

Leaving the single-track West Shore terminus to the strains of 'Auld Lang Syne' from the crowd, No. 4 led No. 8 back to the North Western Hotel and on through the town towards the Little Orme. Here the Chairman of Llandudno UDC, Councillor John Owen, took over the controls for the stretch up to the depot. No. 8 paused here while the controls were handed over to the Mayor of Colwyn Bay, Councillor Edward Hughes, for the final run down to the Greenfield Road terminus, pursued by a wide assortment of other road users. Ex-Accrington No. 3 was quickly substituted for sister car 4 when the depot was reached as one of that car's controllers had failed at the West Shore, meaning that it had had to be driven from the rear end all the way to Rhos! (It seems that No. 3's seat cushions had already been removed for sale as souvenirs and had to be hurriedly put back.) The arrival at, and subsequent departure from, Colwyn Bay were witnessed by another large crowd and a second convoy made its way along behind No. 8, this time returning to the depot which it reached at about 1.00 am. It had been arranged that passengers for Llandudno would be taken on from there by one of the company's buses, though in the event many preferred to walk back along the silent tracks to pay their last respects to the LCBER.

So died the tramway.

The 'Last Car', 24th March, 1956: ex-Bournemouth No. 8 outside the Grand Theatre in Llandudno in the company of No. 3 (ex-Accrington). *Author's Collection*

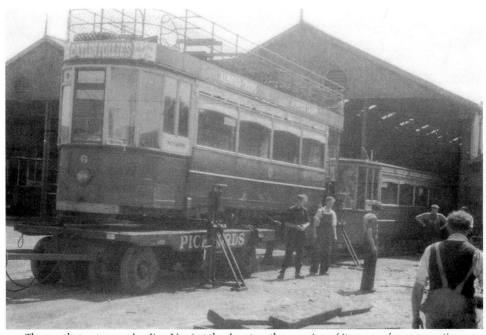

The one that got away: loading No. 6 at the depot on the occasion of its rescue for preservation.
G.R. Thomson Collection

A close-up of one of No. 6's maximum traction trucks.   *G.R. Thomson Collection*

Chapter Eight

Epilogue

Thus it was on Sunday 25th March, 1956 that the LCBER became a bus operator with six second-hand (and rather decrepit) double-deck 'Red Buses' painted dark red and cream - a livery that ironically came close to the tramcars' original maroon and cream - plying their trade between Llandudno and Colwyn Bay, their one service adhering faithfully to the former tramway route and deviating only slightly at the reserved sections of track in Bodafon Fields and Glan-y-Mor Road - and, at the Colwyn Bay end, after half a century finally serving the railway station there via Penryhn Road. Not so faithfully adhered to was the agreement with Crosville over such small things as timetables which, according to the local authorities, residents and press, were chiefly notable by their absence. At first the bus service was every 10 minutes though this was later reduced to 15 minutes as a fuel-saving measure, a result of the Suez Crisis that autumn and winter (and later still to 20 minutes).

By July - in time for the holiday season - the bus fleet had been enlarged to 13 service vehicles, with seven more Guy 'Arab' double-deckers bought from Southdown Motor Services Ltd of Sussex joining the original two Daimler double-deckers from Newcastle-upon-Tyne Corporation and four ex-Southdown Guy Arabs. All were housed in the former tram depot, which had been adapted for the purpose. (A detailed fleet list is given in *Appendix Two*.)

Messrs Walter & Co. of Oldham and Conwy quickly went about their contracted task of dismantling, destroying and generally disposing of the carcase of the tramway. The Tramway Museum Society, a national body formed by enthusiasts just the year before, opened a fund to acquire car No. 6 (formerly Bournemouth No. 85) and Bournemouth Town Council also expressed a willingness to purchase it but if a very generous and big-hearted Mr A. Richardson of Rhyl had not stepped in, paid the asking price of £75 and presented the tram to the Museum of British Transport at Clapham, one wonders if No. 6 would have been saved from the fate of its shedmates. Stripped of anything of scrap value, anything saleable, the bodies were unceremoniously burnt outside the depot. All, that is, except Nos. 23 and 24, the two ex-Darwen cars: their steel bodies survived through the summer before receiving the scrapman's torch when no buyer was found for them as working vehicles. (For information regarding the disposal of many of the saleable parts see *Appendix Three*.)

Although the overhead wires went within a month of the closure, together with the rails from the reserved sections, the rest of the track lingered on - to the considerable annoyance of the Llandudno and Colwyn Bay local authorities who wished to see its speedy removal. The reason for the delay was quite simple: the LCBER did not have the money to pay for the lifting of the track and the subsequent restoration of the roads. The company claimed that if it did decide to lift the track (presumably its scrap value would cover at least part of the cost of this operation) it saw no reason to make good the roads since -

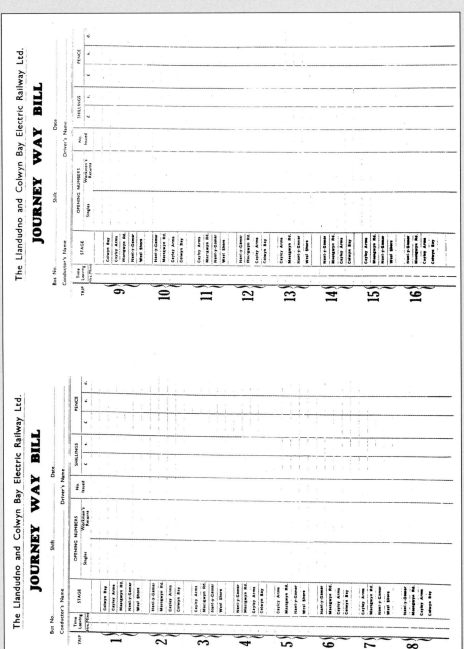

Way bill as used by the company's bus crews following the tramway's closure.

undeniably - their condition in that broken state would still be better than it was in 1906! The two councils were not unnaturally inclined to a somewhat different view and began to make threatening noises regarding the seeking of powers to lift the track, repair the roads and present the company with the bill - whereupon the company decided not to go down fighting and handed over £5,000 to the councils to do the whole job though, as was the case with their counterparts elsewhere in the country, they were content to simply tar over most sections of track to save disrupting traffic, only removing the rails years later, in piecemeal fashion, when roadworks compelled it.

The process of making good the roads occasioned minor alterations to the company's bus route and services, though greater problems arose from the competition with Crosville and the far smaller concern soon found itself being squeezed out of existence. In April 1961 the company announced that it was giving up the struggle on this front as well and the last LCBER buses ran on Saturday 27th May, by which date another three Guy 'Arabs' had been added to the fleet as replacement vehicles (and a programme of converting some of the fleet to open-toppers had begun). The next day the service was taken over by Crosville, who had purchased the company's goodwill for £40,000.

There was now little reason for the continuing existence of the LCBER. All that was left of the business was the Penrhyn Bay toll road - and after the toll gate attendant fell ill and was not replaced (about April 1961), even that revenue had dried up. In the face of the local authorities' desire to improve the public roads in the area to serve growing residential development, the company decided to dispose of its remaining assets. Accordingly, on 14th November, 1961 the LCBER went into voluntary liquidation, paying to its shareholders 10s. per 10s. preferred share and ¼d. per 1s. deferred share. The company's Directors at the close were Messrs Amphlett, Baker and Dodman; Dodman had been Chairman since Nall retired in 1958, and Baker had become a Director the year before that.

Today the urban development that took place during the tramway's life continues unabated; Llandudno's housing estates now extend out alongside the route of the line to the West Parade and to Craig-y-Don. As so often happens with tramways, as opposed to railways, traces of their erstwhile existence disappear quickly after they are closed and the case of the LCBER is no exception. At the end of Gloddaeth Avenue, though, the former West Shore terminus is marked by the continuing presence of the former bus and tram shelter, a circular cast-iron and glass structure believed to date from 1910 (and recently renovated). Moving on, the street sections of the tramway are now just streets, with no hint that they were once more than that, whilst the reserved sections have undergone a variety of changes. The Bodafon Fields right of way became a path across the pasture from which it was taken with only a fence, a hedge along one side of the decaying trackbed and the odd sleeper and uprooted, sawn-off traction pole to indicate where the trams once ran; a metal gate marked the point where trams crossed Nant-y-Gamar Road to begin their ascent of the Little Orme. Today the path is an access road to the Bodafon Farm Park.

On the far side of Bodafon Fields, where the reserved section reached Bryn-y-Bia Road, the trackbed has houses built upon it, whilst the roadway section

The refurbished LCBER office building and waiting room beside the former car shed, 1992.

M. Donnison

Looking towards the West Shore, 1992; little has changed since the 1920s except the size of the trees - and the traffic.   *M. Donnison*

over the summit and the reserved section on the descent of Penrhyn Hill have suffered even more: the construction of a split-level dual carriageway in 1971, and other major changes to the roadways in this area, have completely obliterated the former trackbed. Glan-y-Mor Road is now bordered by houses, the roadway continuing along the coast by the new sea wall where the old toll road and trackbed were. In Rhos, behind an extended frontage, the former car shed enjoyed a new lease of life as a parcels depot after the tramway's bus service ceased; the general office too survived, though in a much rebuilt form. Sadly, after surviving half a century since the end of the tramway, the site was cleared in the spring of 2006 to make way for a housing development, putting paid to recent hopes of using the buildings as a community/visitors' centre. With the demolition of the depot, Colwyn Bay has seen the erasure of all traces of the line that once served it so well.

The story of the closure of the LCBER cannot be left there, for there is a matter no account of the tramway's life can avoid. For the past 50 years two questions have been asked, time and time again, by almost everyone with an interest in the tramway: who was to blame for the closure, and could it have been prevented? To try and find an answer to the first question is, at best, to misunderstand the historical context and, at worst, to embark on a witch-hunt. Even though specific individuals undoubtedly took specific decisions that led to the line's closure, tramway history tells us that those decisions would have been somehow arrived at anyway, for by 1956 the age of the tramway in the British Isles was to all intents and purposes over, at least for the foreseeable future. In 1956, the only comparable line then still operational in Great Britain was that linking Blackpool and Fleetwood on the Lancashire coast. This however was municipally-owned and run very much as a tourist amenity, not as a commercial enterprise; indeed, that part of the once-extensive system serving the town behind the one main seafront route had been gradually abandoned. Llandudno UDC, operator of the Great Orme Tramway since 1949 to no great financial advantage, was hardly disposed to take on the burden of the loss-making, road-cluttering anachronism that was the LCBER. Circumstances, not individuals, were responsible for the tramway's closure.

Could the tramway have been saved? The harsh answer is a resounding 'No'. It has often been claimed that an enthusiasts-backed plan proposed at the time, to buy the LCBER and run it with volunteers, could have worked if given the chance. The simple truth is that it would never have been given that chance. The railway preservation movement was then still very much in its infancy (the Talyllyn Railway had operated in its new, preserved guise only since 1951) and was regarded with suspicion - and doubts as to its viability - in many quarters; crucially, it could in no way serve as a model for tramway operation as the latter involved running electric vehicles along busy urban thoroughfares with a myriad of associated safety implications. However well-financed, skilled and well-meaning the volunteers, however possible the idea was in theory - and it was - local and national authorities would simply not have countenanced such a scheme at that time. They would not today in Llandudno, Colwyn Bay or anywhere else. The closure of the LCBER was inevitable, its resurrection impossible.

The former reserved section through Bodafon Fields, 1992, with Nant-y-Gamar Road in the foreground and the Little Orme in the distance.   *Author*

The former toll road on an overcast day in late 1992 with the new sea wall on the left and the entrance to the golf club on the right.   *Author*

Left: The notice boards at the Rhos end of the toll road. Note the officially-correct reference to 'light railway' rather than 'tramway' or even 'electric railway'.

D.W.K. Jones

Below: Trams no more: the pair of surviving destination boards on display in the National Tramway Museum, Crich. *M. Donnison*

There the story of the LCBER appeared to end with the tramway becoming a fading memory for all who had known it. But it does not quite end there: on 19th September, 1974 the Llandudno Tramway Society was formed to keep that memory alive by collecting relics of the line for an intended local museum. Although the Society's plan to secure the return of car No. 6 to Llandudno was defeated when Bournemouth made a successful application for custody of it following the 1973 closure of the Museum of British Transport at Clapham, the remains of ex-Northampton double-decker No. 21 were rescued from a Northamptonshire farm in 1977 and moved to North Wales, the idea being to restore it to operational condition for use - at some future date - on a new or relaid section of tramway in Llandudno. In October of the same year a quantity of original rails from the West Shore terminus was lifted by the new local authority, Aberconwy Borough Council, and sold to the Society. (Some 20 years later the pointwork outside Woolworths at the end of the Hooson's Corner loop was dug up by Welsh Water and presented to Llandudno Museum in Gloddaeth Street, to join its tramway display.)

Since that optimistic beginning, the Society has had a long, hard struggle keeping its dream alive, encompassing several changes of name, aim, fortune and premises along the way - a struggle eerily reminiscent of that of the formative years of the LCBER itself! The current position is that, after reconstitution in 1997 as the Llandudno & Colwyn Bay Tramway Society, its principal short-term objective has been the establishment of a local museum embracing the whole transport history of the area, not just of the LCBER, so as to capture the widest support and patronage; disappointingly, this cannot be in the former depot. The Society now possesses the bodies of former Bournemouth double-deckers No. 86 (sister car to LCBER 6 and renumbered 7 by the Society) and No. 126 (sister car to the LCBER's other ex-Bournemouth trams), and its mid- to long-term objective is the construction of an off-road, working tramway on which they could be operated, possibly linking Bodafon Fields with Llandudno promenade, possibly as a pleasure line on the West Shore.

In 1996 a more ambitious plan, for a commercial tramway through Llandudno along the route of the LCBER, was announced by Mostyn Estates Ltd, the major local landowner. This was to have operated as a low-cost 'park and ride' scheme to ferry visitors from Bodafon Fields into the town centre, using flywheel-powered, stored-energy vehicles (Parry People Movers) as developed by J.P.M. Parry & Associates Ltd of Cradley Heath in the West Midlands. Alas, the scheme was not proceeded with: after a promising start, with much official support and some funding in place, by 2001 it had been blocked by political opponents (and an antipathy by some residents towards the modern styling of the proposed tramcars), though a variety of similar ones have been, and are being, tested elsewhere on both narrow and standard gauge lines. The project is not dead but on hold - and who knows? Perhaps one day in the not-too-distant future the Queen of Welsh watering-places will echo once more to the sound of metal wheels on metal rails, and visitors will once again be able to savour the delights of an open-top tram-ride beside the sea.

Chapter Nine

Operations

Services

The tramway's very first timetable, which came into effect from the line's opening, showed services commencing from both ends (West Parade and Rhos Depot) at 9.00 am and operating at 30-minute intervals. (Until the extension of the line into Colwyn Bay in 1908 passengers between there and Rhos were conveyed at 3*d*. a time in horse-brakes by Messrs J.F. Francis & Sons, carriage proprietors of Colwyn Bay, under an agreement with the tramway company.) The journey time over this first section of the line opened was approximately 30 minutes; with the extension to Colwyn Bay this increased to 40 minutes, and again to 50 minutes when Old Colwyn was reached in 1915. After closure of this last extension the journey time reverted to roughly 40 minutes - actual times of different scheduled workings varied by a few minutes. Departure times from a few of the intermediate stops were quoted on public timetables, and several of the intermediate stops boasted small wooden shelters for waiting passengers - shelters which were often, in later years, made from parts of dismantled tramcars.

When fully operational (from November 1907 onwards) the tramway's normal pattern of working was a 10-minute interval service in the summer, reduced to a 20-minute one in the winter months (though during the 1930s a 15-minute winter, 10-minute spring and a 6-minute summer service was in force). Services were generally rather more frequent on Saturdays and less so (and more limited) on Sundays. Interspersed with these through workings were the two 'locals': shuttle services between the West Parade and Nant-y-Gamar Road in Llandudno, and between the depot and the eastern terminus; these helped free-up spaces on the end-to-end cars.

Scheduled services normally commenced between 6.00 and 7.00 am and finished between 10.00 and 11.00 pm (though as with the actual schedules, these times were subject to endless minor variations over the years but serve to give the general picture). The first car of the day was a workmen's special: under the 1898 Order the company was obliged to run at least one car in each direction every day (except Sundays) before 7.00 am and again after 5.30 pm for the benefit of workmen, who were to travel at a reduced rate. (This was a standard provision of tramway Orders and Acts, affording manual workers, shop assistants and the like the opportunity to use this new and advantageous mode of public transport at times convenient for them.)

Occasionally special charter trips were run over the line, usually for children's outings in the early years and in later years for tramway enthusiasts wishing to ride the tramway before it closed.

Brake adjustments being made by one of the tramway's fitters, outside the depot.

G.R. Thomson

One of the ex-Darwen double-deckers manoeuvring in the depot entrance.   *D.W.K. Jones*

Ex-Bournemouth No. 13, in service, passing toastrack No. 21, working the 1951 Light Railway Transport League special, in Glan-y-Mor Road. *D.W.K. Jones*

Ex-Bournemouth No. 8 on Penrhyn Hill. *Provenance Unknown*

Hooson's Corner, August 1955, with open-topper No. 13 screeching to a halt. Note the distinctive Woolworth's lettering of the period behind the car.   *John Edgington*

'Spiv' No. 24 in Rhos depot, with sister car No. 23 behind next to toastrack No. 21.

D.W.K. Jones

Working

As would be expected, different patterns of working were in force at different times of the year, and as more cars were bought. In post-1936 summers all the double-deckers would be in service, together with the open toastracks so beloved of holidaymakers, while the single-deckers stayed in reserve. At the height of the season the whole fleet would be in action and on very busy days inspectors would often terminate cars from Colwyn Bay at Hooson's Corner in an attempt to keep them to some semblance of a timetable, with passengers for the West Shore then having to wait for another tram to take them on. During the summer season peak additional 'jumper' conductors were employed in Llandudno to ride the crowded trams for a few stops, collecting fares, before jumping off and catching one going the other way, so easing the burden on the regular conductors. In all, some 20 (pre-World War II) or 30 (post-war) seasonal staff were employed to supplement the tramway's 60-odd full-time employees.

The reduced winter services were handled by the single-deckers until the arrival of the double-deckers, which then generally took over, though in the tramway's final years a decline in out of season traffic numbers meant that the single-deckers largely replaced them in the winter months.

Generally speaking, each car - crewed by a driver and a conductor (or conductress) - would adhere to the timetable as far as possible; this usually meant a fairly continuous service, throughout the day, from one terminus to the other then almost immediately back again.

Fares

The LCBER's original fare structure, for single fares as laid down by the 1898 Order, was based upon a maximum rate of 1*d*. per mile or fraction thereof, though the company was permitted to charge 2*d*. for any distance between ½ mile and two miles. The exception to this was the workmen's rate of ½*d*. per mile (minimum fare 1*d*.). Passengers were allowed 28 lb. of accompanying luggage free of charge; other set rates could be applied at the discretion of the company for various commodities, the tramway being authorized to carry minerals, parcels, animals and general goods in addition to passengers.

This fare structure gave a basic end-to-end fare of 5*d*. when the first section of the line opened, with this going up to to 8*d*. when the line was fully opened. During the late 1920s fare increases were authorized (up to 1½*d*. per mile ordinary, 1*d*. per mile workmen's and an extra 75 per cent on the goods charges) but overall the changes had little effect. Indeed, the through fare later dropped to 7*d*. and was raised to 9*d*. only in 1953. Apart from these changes - and minor stage alterations - the fares were remarkably consistent throughout the life of the tramway. One bone of contention for local residents, however, was that after the line was cut back to Greenfield Road in 1930, the stage structure in force meant that passengers were charged an extra 1*d*. between there and St Paul's church, resulting in cars running virtually empty over this short section (apart from at the height of the summer season). The company thereupon unofficially

LLANDUDNO AND COLWYN BAY ELECTRIC RAILWAY LIMITED

SUMMER TIME TABLE

COLWYN BAY (Greenfield Road) TO LLANDUDNO (West Shore)

MONDAYS TO SATURDAYS

		am	am	am	am	am	am	am	am		pm	pm	pm	pm	pm	pm	pm
COLWYN BAY (St. Paul's Church)	dept.	...	7 12	7 27	7 42	7 57	8 12	...	8 32		10 2	10 12	10 22	10 32	10 42	10 52	11 2
* King's Road	,,	...	7 16	7 31	7 46	8 1	8 16	...	8 35	Then every 10 mins. until	10 5	10 14	10 24	10 34	10 44	10 54	11 4
RHOS (Cayley Promenade)	,,	6 50	7 19	7 34	7 49	8 4	8 19	...	8 39		10 9	10 18	10 28	10 38	10 48	10 58	11 8
* Church Road	,,	6 52	7 21	7 36	7 51	8 6	8 21	8 30	8 41		10 11	10 20	10 30	10 40	10 50	11 0	11 10
PENRHYN BAY (Golf Club)	,,	6 54	7 23	7 38	7 53	8 8	8 23	8 33	8 43		10 13	...	...				
* Little Orme Cafe	,,	6 56	7 25	7 40	7 55	8 10	8 25	8 36	8 46		10 16						
LLANDUDNO (Queen's Road)	,,	7 4	7 34	7 49	8 4	8 19	8 34	8 45	8 55		10 25						
* West Shore	arr.	7 11	7 41	7 56	8 11	8 26	8 41	8 53	9 3		10 33						

SUNDAYS

		am	am	am	am	am	am	am	am	am	am	am		pm	pm	pm	pm
COLWYN BAY (St. Paul's Church)	dept.	...	...	8 32	...	8 52	9 2	9 12	9 22	9 32	9 42	9 52		9 52	10 2	10 12	10 32
* King's Road	,,			8 35		8 55	9 5	9 15	9 25	9 35	9 45	9 55	Then every 10 mins. until	9 55	10 5	10 15	10 35
RHOS (Cayley Promenade)	,,	8 8	8 29	8 39	8 49	8 59	9 9	9 19	9 29	9 39	9 49	9 59		9 58	10 8	10 18	10 38
* Church Road	,,	8 11	8 31	8 41	8 51	9 1	9 11	9 21	9 31	9 41	9 51	10 -1		10 0	10 10	10 20	10 40
PENRHYN BAY (Golf Club)	,,	8 13	8 33	8 43	8 53	9 3	9 13	9 23	9 33	9 43	9 53	10 3		...			
* Little Orme Cafe	,,	8 16	8 36	8 46	8 56	9 6	9 16	9 26	9 36	9 46	9 56	10 6		...			
LLANDUDNO (Queen's Road)	,,	8 25	8 45	8 55	9 5	9 15	9 25	9 35	9 45	9 55	10 5	10 15		...			
* West Shore	arr.	8 33	8 53	9 3	9 13	9 23	9 33	9 43	9 53	10 3	10 13	10 23		...			

LLANDUDNO (West Shore) TO COLWYN BAY (Greenfield Road)

MONDAYS TO SATURDAYS

		am	am	am	am	am	am	am	am	am	am	am		pm	pm	pm
LLANDUDNO (West Shore)	dept.	...	...	7 13	...	7 43	7 58	8 13	...	8 28	8 43	...	8 55	10 15	10 25	10 35
* Queen's Road	,,			7 20		7 50	8 5	8 20		8 35	8 50		9 3	10 23	10 32	10 42
* Little Orme Cafe	,,			7 27		7 57	8 13	8 27		8 43	8 57		9 12	10 32	10 39	10 49
PENRHYN BAY (Golf Club)	,,			7 29		7 59	8 16	8 29		8 46	8 59		9 15	10 35	10 41	10 51
* Church Road	,,	7 0	7 15	7 31	7 45	8 1	8 18	8 31	8 40	8 48	9 1	9 10	9 18	10 38	10 43	10 53
RHOS (Cayley Promenade)	,,	7 3	7 18	7 33	7 48	8 3	8 21	8 33	8 43	8 51	9 3	9 12	9 21	10 41	10 46	10 56
* King's Road	,,	7 6	7 21	7 36	7 51	8 6	8 25	8 36	8 46	8 54	9 6	9 15	9 24	10 44	10 49	...
COLWYN BAY (Penrhyn Road)	arr.	7 9	7 24	7 39	7 54	8 9	8 28	8 39	8 49	8 58	9 9	9 18	9 28	10 48	10 52	...

SUNDAYS

		am	am	am	am	am	am	am	am	am	am	am		pm	pm	pm	pm
LLANDUDNO (West Shore)	dept.	...	...	8 35	...	8 55	9 5	9 15	9 25	9 35	9 45			9 45	9 55	10 5	10 15
* Queen's Road	,,			8 43		9 3	9 13	9 23	9 33	9 43	9 53		Then every 10 mins. until	9 53	10 3	10 13	10 23
* Little Orme Cafe	,,			8 52		9 12	9 22	9 32	9 42	9 52	10 2			10 2	10 12	10 22	10 32
PENRHYN BAY (Golf Club)	,,			8 55		9 15	9 25	9 35	9 45	9 55	10 5			10 4	10 15	10 24	10 34
* Church Road	,,	8 20	8 40	8 50	8 58	9 10	9 18	9 28	9 38	9 48	9 58	10 8		10 6	10 18	10 26	10 36
RHOS (Cayley Promenade)	,,	8 22	8 42	8 52	9 1	9 12	9 21	9 31	9 41	9 51	10 1	10 11		10 9	10 21	10 28	10 38
* King's Road	,,	8 26	8 46	8 56	9 4	9 16	9 26	9 36	9 44	9 54	10 4	10 14		10 24	...		
COLWYN BAY (Penrhyn Road)	arr.	8 30	8 50	9 0	9 8	9 20	9 28	9 38	9 48	9 58	10 8	10 18		10 28	...		

* The Company shall not be responsible for any delay or inconvenience due to any variations of the above Time Table.
  Departure times from these stopping places are shown for the convenience of passengers and are approximate only.

W. BUTTERWORTH,
General Manager.

POWLSONS, PRINTERS, COLWYN BAY

LCBER summer timetable for its replacement bus service, undated. (Butterworth was the tramway's last General Manager.)

LLANDUDNO AND COLWYN BAY ELECTRIC RAILWAY LIMITED
WINTER TIME TABLE

COLWYN BAY (Greenfield Road) TO LLANDUDNO (West Shore)

MONDAYS TO SATURDAYS

		am	am	am	am	am	am	am	am	am	am	am	am	am	am	am	am	am	am
Greenfield Road	dept.	...	7 10	7 25	7 40	7 55	8 10	8 30	8 40	8 50	9 0	...	9 20	...	9 40	...	10 0	...	10 10
St. Paul's Church	,,	...	7 12	7 27	7 42	7 57	8 12	8 32	8 42	8 52	9 2	...	9 22	...	9 42	...	10 2	...	10 12
Rhos Promenade	,,	...	7 18	7 32	7 47	8 2	8 17	8 37	8 49	8 58	9 8	...	9 28	...	9 48	...	10 8	...	10 18
Church Road	arr.	6 50	...	...	...	...	...	...	...	8 59	...	...	...	...	...	...	...	...	10 19
Nant-y-Gismar Road	dept.	...	...	...	...	...	...	...	...	...	...	9 25	...	9 45	...	10 5	...	10 25	...
Queen's Road	,,	7 4	7 33	7 42	3 3	8 18	8 33	8 55	9 4	...	9 22	9 26	9 42	9 46	10 2	10 6	10 22	10 26	...
Palladium Corner	arr.	...	...	...	...	...	...	...	...	...	9 28	...	9 48	...	10 8	...	10 28	...	...
West Shore	arr.	7 11	7 41	7 56	8 11	8 26	8 41	9 3	9 12	...	9 34	...	9 54	...	10 14	...	10 34		

MONDAYS TO SATURDAYS

		am	am	am	am	am		pm	pm	pm	pm	pm	pm	pm	pm	pm	pm	pm	pm	pm	pm	pm
Greenfield Road	dept.	10 20	...	10 30	10 40	10 50		6 10	6 20	6 30	6 40	7 0	7 35	8 5	8 35	9 5	9 35	10 5				
St. Paul's Church	,,	10 22	...	10 32	10 42	10 50		6 12	6 22	6 32	6 42	7 2	7 37	8 7	8 37	9 7	9 37	10 7				
Rhos Promenade	,,	10 28	...	10 38	10 48	10 58		6 18	6 28	6 38	6 48	7 8	7 42	8 12	8 42	9 13	9 43	10 13				
Church Road	,,	...	...	10 39	...	10 59	Repeated each hour until	6 19	6 29	6 39	6 49	7 9	7 43	8 13	8 43	9 14	9 44	10 14				
Nant-y-Gamar Road	dept.	...	10 45	...	...	...		...	...	...	...	...	...	...	...	...	...	...				
Queen's Road	,,	10 42	10 46	...	11 2	...		6 45	...	...	7 2	7 26	7 56	8 26	8 56	9 26	9 56					
Palladium Corner	arr.	10 48	...	...	11 8	...		6 51	...	...	7 8	...	...	...	...	...	...					
West Shore	arr.	...	...	10 54	...	...		6 53	...	...	7 33	8 3	8 33	9 3	9 33	10 3						

LLANDUDNO (West Shore) TO COLWYN BAY (Greenfield Road)

MONDAYS TO SATURDAYS

		am	am	am	am	am	am	am	am	am	am	am	am	am
West Shore	dept.	...	...	7 13	...	7 43	7 58	...	8 13	8 28	8 45	9 5	9 15	...	9 35	...	8 55	...
Palladium Corner	,,	...	...	...	...	...	...	...	...	...	...	...	9 17	9 37	9 49	9 57
Queen's Road	,,	...	...	7 20	...	7 50	8 5	...	8 20	8 36	8 53	9 13	9 23	9 38	9 45	8 55	10 3
Nant-y-Gamar Road	arr.	...	...	...	...	...	...	...	...	...	...	...	9 24	...	9 44	...	10 4
Church Road	dept.	6 55	7 10	...	7 45	...	8 25	...	...	...	...	...	...	...	...	9 55
Rhos Promenade	,,	7 0	7 15	7 32	7 47	8 2	8 21	8 31	8 41	8 51	9 9	9 31	...	9 51	...	10 1	10 11	10 20
Railway Station, C. Bay	arr.	7 8	7 23	7 38	7 53	8 8	8 27	8 37	8 47	8 57	9 17	9 38	...	9 58	...	10 10	10 18	10 21	10 28

MONDAYS TO SATURDAYS

		am	am	am	am	am		pm	pm	pm	pm	pm	pm	pm	pm	pm	pm	pm
West Shore	dept.	...	...	10 15	...	...		5 55	...	6 55	...	...	7 35	8 5	8 35	9 5	9 35	10 5
Palladium Corner	,,	10 9	10 17	...	10 29	...		...	6 6	6 29	6 57	7 9	7 37	8 7	8 37	9 7	9 37	Waits for Cinema
Queen's Road	,,	10 15	10 23	...	10 35	...	Repeated each hour until	6 15	6 35	7 3	7 15	7 42	8 12	8 42	9 12	9 42	10 12
Nant-y-Gamar Road	arr.	...	10 24	...	...	...		...	...	...	...	...	...	...	...	...
Church Road	dept.	...	...	10 40	...	...		6 20	6 20	...	7 30	...	...	...	...	...	10 25
Rhos Promenade	,,	10 31	...	10 41	10 51		6 21	6 31	...	7 21	...	7 56	8 26	8 56	9 26	9 56	
Railway Station, C. Bay	arr.	10 38	...	10 48	10 58		6 28	6 38	6 58	7 28	8 3	8 33	9 3	9 33	10 3	

COLWYN BAY to LLANDUDNO
SUNDAYS

		am	am	am	am		pm	pm	pm		pm	pm	pm
Greenfield Road	dept.	...	9 45	10 15	10 45	And every 30 mins. until	1 50	2 20		9 20	9 50	10 20
St. Paul's Church	,,	...	9 47	10 17	10 47		1 52	2 22		9 22	9 52	10 22
Rhos Promenade	,,	9 24	9 52	10 22	10 52		1 57	2 27	And every 30 mins. until	9 27	9 57	10 27
Queen's Road	,,	9 36	10 6	10 36	11 6		2 11	2 41		9 41	Depot only
West Shore	arr.	9 43	10 13	10 43	11 13		2 18	2 48		9 48	

LLANDUDNO to COLWYN BAY
SUNDAYS

		am	am	am	am		pm	pm	pm		pm	pm
West Shore	dept.	...	9 45	10 15	10 45	And every 30 minutes until	1 50	2 20	2 50		9 20	9 50
Queen's Road	,,	...	9 52	10 22	10 52		1 57	2 27	2 57	And every 30 minutes until	9 27	9 57
Rhos Promenade	,,	9 35	10 6	10 36	11 6		2 11	2 41	3 11		9 41	10 11
Railway Stn., C. Bay	arr.	9 42	10 13	10 43	11 13		2 18	2 48	3 18		9 48	10 18

TO OPERATE FROM 3rd SUNDAY IN SEPTEMBER UNTIL SATURDAY BEFORE WHIT-SUNDAY

The Company shall not be responsible for any delay or inconvenience due to any variations of the above Time Table. Departure times from these stopping places are shown for the convenience of passengers and are approximate only.

POWLSONS, PRINTERS, COLWYN BAY

N. BUTTERWORTH,
General Manager.

A similar-looking winter timetable, probably of the same period. Note that - at last! - Colwyn Bay railway station is served by the company.

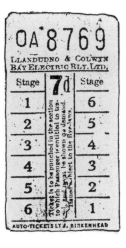

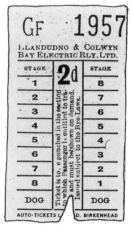

A selection of LCBER single tickets with sample advertisements as printed on the reverse. Colours used were: 1d. white, 1½d. brown (later brick red), 2d. buff, 3d. blue, 4d. yellow, 5d. green, 6d. mauve, 7d. pink, 8d. purple, 9d. light brick red.

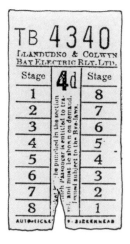

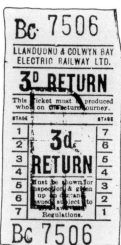

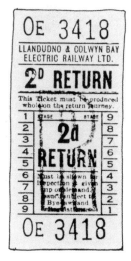

More tramway tickets (again, all by Auto-Tickets Ltd of Birkenhead) including 2*d*. (grey) and 3*d*. (white) returns.

LLANDUDNO & COLWYN BAY ELECTRIC RAILWAY LIMITED

LLANDUDNO - PENRHYN BAY - RHOS-ON-SEA - COLWYN BAY

SINGLE FARES

```
1/1  11  10   9   7½  —   6½  5½  4   3½  2   —   2    LLANDUDNO (West Shore)
     11  10   9   7½  6½  —   5½  4   3   2   —   —        PALLADIUM or ST. JOHN'S CORNER / CHURCH
     —   —   —   5½  —   4   —   —   2                 NORTH WESTERN HOTEL
         10   9   7½  6½  5½  —   3   2                 QUEEN'S ROAD or CARMEN SYLVA ROAD
              9   7½  6½  5½  4   3   2                 QUEEN'S ROAD or NANT-Y-GAMAR ROAD
                  7½  6½  5½  4   3   2                 BRYN-Y-BIA ROAD (Llandudno Road End)
                      —   5½  4   3   2                 PENRHYNSIDE
                          5½  4   3   2                 LITTLE ORME CAFE
                              6½  4   3   2             PENRHYN BAY (Maesgwyn Road)
                                  4   3   2             CHURCH ROAD
                                      4   3   2         RHOS-ON-SEA (Cayley Promenade or Colwyn Avenue)
                                          3   2         FIVEWAYS or KING'S ROAD
                                              2         COLWYN BAY (Bay View Road or Greenfield Road)
```

WORKERS' DAILY RETURN FARES

```
1/3  1/4  1/2  1/0  11  10  7  —      LLANDUDNO (West Shore)
1/4  1/3  1/2  1/1  10  —              PALLADIUM CORNER or ST. JOHN'S CHURCH
1/3  1/2  1/1  11   7   —              QUEEN'S ROAD or NANT-Y-GAMAR ROAD
1/1  11   10   7                       BRYN-Y-BIA ROAD (Llandudno Road End)
1/0  10   7    —                       PENRHYNSIDE
     11   —                            MAESGWYN ROAD
     —    —                            CHURCH ROAD
     —    —                            COLWYN AVENUE or CAYLEY PROMENADE
          —                            FIVEWAYS or KING'S ROAD
                                       COLWYN BAY (Bay View Road or Greenfield Road)
```

Return Tickets at Workpeople's Fare rates are available to any bona-fide person travelling to work and scheduled to complete their journey at or before 8.0 a.m. The return journey may be taken at any time of the day. Workpeople's Tickets are not available on Sundays.

CHILDREN'S FARES

Children under FIVE years of age FREE, if not occupying a seat, accompanied by an Adult Fare Paying Passenger, providing that not more than one such child accompanies any passenger. Additional children, irrespective of age, MUST BE PAID FOR.

Children from 5 up to their 14th birthday half fare (unless otherwise stated), and also, bona fide children up to their 16th birthday during term time only and then only to and from school, Sundays excepted, can travel at HALF ORDINARY FARES. Minimum Children's Fare 1d. Half-penny is treated as penny except in the case of the following adults fares, when the children's fare will be:—

Adult	Children
2d.	1d.
3d.	1½d.
4d.	2d.
5d.	2½d.
6d.	3d.
7d.	3½d.
8d.	4d.

SCHOLARS' 5-DAY WEEKLY TICKETS

Scholars' 5-Day Weekly Tickets are issued by Conductors between any two stages on Mondays and Tuesdays up to 2.0 p.m., where indicated on Fare Tables.

Scholars' Weekly Tickets are available during week of issue only for two outward and two inward journeys each day.

These tickets are available to bona-fide school children up to their 16th birthday (during term time only), and then only, to and from school.

Where the ordinary Adult Single Fares are:	Scholars' 5-Day Weekly Tickets are:
2	1/8
2½	1/10
3	2/1
3½	2/3
4	2/5
5	2/11
5½	3/0
6	3/4
6½	3/6
7½	4/1
9	4/10
10	5/11

W. BUTTERWORTH,

General Manager.

An undated concessionary fares table (probably early 1950s).

abandoned this stretch - and tarred over the rails - until about 1937 when it gave in, reinstated the section and dropped the higher fare.

Children under 14 years of age travelled at half-price; children under three rode free. Special weekly tickets for schoolchildren and workmen were issued, as well as workmen's day returns and, until 1941, a special 'excursion' return of 1s. was available between Llandudno and Colwyn Bay. Tickets used were of the Bell Punch variety (with punches supplied by Alfred Williamson Ltd).

Tolls

Mention should be made of the tolls charged by the LCBER on its toll road section of the tramway along Penrhyn Bay. These tolls, for a return journey on the day of ticket issue only, were as follows:

	s.	d.
Perambulator, light handcart or pedal cycle		1
Motor cycle on two wheels carrying one person		3
Motor cycle combination, or carrying two persons		6
Motor vehicle of seating capacity not exceeding eight passengers	1	0
Cart or carriage drawn by one horse	1	0
Light lorry or van not exceeding 5 tons gross loaded	1	0
Cart or carriage drawn by two horses	1	6

Heavy lorries, coaches and public service vehicles (PSVs) were barred from using the toll road; however, when the company's own motor buses replaced the trams they used the road and from then on other PSVs were admitted for a toll of 2s. 6d. The notice at the toll-booth listing the above charges also gave the following instruction:

Drivers of vehicles passing through this gate are respectfully requested to see that the Toll-gate Keeper punches, in their presence, a ticket representing the value of the toll paid.

Accidents

There is no reason to suppose that the LCBER was not without its fair share of minor accidents; it does appear, though, to have been unlucky in being involved in at least four fatal ones, of which three were well documented at the time. The first of these occurred on Friday 3rd July, 1914 when 10-year-old Trevor Roberts, of Penryhn Bay, was knocked down by a tram outside the golf club at Rhos. Trevor was employed after school hours as a caddie at the club and on the evening in question he walked out from behind a waiting tram and was hit by an approaching one, apparently disregarding (or misinterpreting) the warning bell that rang in the clubhouse whenever a tram approached.

The second incident involved a Holyhead woman, Dorothy Wall, who slipped and fractured her skull while trying to avoid a tram in Craig-y-Don on the evening of Thursday 9th February, 1928. The third fatality was again that of a child: this time a three-year-old boy, struck by a tram in Penrhyn Avenue on Friday 15th May, 1936 as he ran after his ball. The tram was only travelling at 10 mph but for a three-year-old, that was too much.

Rhos depot with the tramway's horse-drawn tower wagon in the foreground and a toastrack inside the carshed.   *Courtesy Llandudno & Colwyn Bay Tramway Society*

The depressing scene outside the depot at the time of the closure, with an assortment of cars waiting to be scrapped.   *D.W.K. Jones*

Chapter Ten

Rolling Stock

As should be clear from the preceding chapters, the passenger cars used on the LCBER fell into three distinct groups. The first of these comprised the two ex-Canvey Island cars used for testing the line (but never for public service), the second group was made up of the 22 cars ordered new for the line at various dates between 1907 and 1920 whilst the third consisted of the 17 second-hand vehicles purchased between 1932 and 1948 from three different municipal tramway operators: Accrington, Bournemouth and Darwen.

All three groups are dealt with below in the above order, followed by notes on their livery and indicators. A final section deals with the tramway's works cars.

Ex-Canvey Island Cars

The first cars to run on the LCBER were the pair obtained in 1907 from the defunct Canvey Island Electric Tramways. These had been constructed in 1904 by the Brush Electrical Engineering Co. Ltd of Loughborough and were of a standard closed single-decker design. The 17 ft-long saloon body (25 ft 6 in. over fenders) was mounted on a Brush type 'A' truck with 30 in. diameter wheels on a 6 ft wheelbase. Seating was for 26 on two longitudinal seats down the sides of the saloon.

When the Canvey Island venture ground to a halt in the same year that it got underway - 1904 - its stock of four cars was returned to Brush whence two were borrowed, in January 1907, by Bruce Peebles for testing the Llandudno line so far constructed. Later the same year they were returned to their maker, never having been numbered or used in revenue service at Llandudno either. After standing in Brush's works yard for several years they were finally broken up during World War I for their reusable components.

Original Cars Nos. 1-14

The LCBER's first 14 cars of its own were ordered and supplied in one batch for the opening of the line in 1907. Their bodies were constructed by the Midland Railway Carriage & Wagon Co. Ltd of Shrewsbury and the running gear manufactured and fitted by Mountain & Gibson Ltd of Bury. The bodies were long, single-deck saloons with monitor (clerestory) roofs and vestibuled end platforms with entrances each side. Internally the saloon was divided into two compartments, both with longitudinal rattan seating and polished oak and mahogany decor; total accommodation was given as for 42 passengers. The original designation was one compartment for smokers and one for non-smokers but this arrangement was later dropped. (Judging by complaints made

One of the original 1907 cars, now with its side lettering applied but still with its single trolley pole and no roof boards, posed for a publicity photo before the opening of the line.
Courtesy N.B. Traction Collection

A rare picture of the 1920s trials of 1907 car No. 14 with a bow collector fitted at one end - presumably intended to eliminate de-wirements.

Courtesy Llandudno & Colwyn Bay Tramway Society

No. 17 of 1907 (the renumbered 11) in the yard on 21st May, 1951; by this date only two of these original cars survived.   *D.W.K. Jones*

A close-up view of a Mountain & Gibson truck from one of the 1907 cars, removed for servicing in the depot sometime during the 1920s.   *Courtesy Llandudno & Colwyn Bay Tramway Society*

The same truck - or another of the same type - seen from another angle, showing its single motor in its mountings.   *Courtesy Llandudno & Colwyn Bay Tramway Society*

Another view of a Mountain & Gibson equal-wheel truck, this time under 1907 car No. 17 (formerly 11). *D.W.K. Jones*

The saloon interior of No. 17 (ex-11 of 1907) with the large hand-wheel to operate the wheel brakes visible at the far end. *D.W.K. Jones*

Renumbered cars Nos. 17 and 18 of 1907 at Rhos depot in 1952.   *H.L. Runnett*

by members of the public at the time, the communicating door between the two compartments was often left open, or the division simply ignored anyway.)

Running gear consisted of a pair of four-wheel bogie trucks of the equal-wheel, swing bolster type, with two Bruce Peebles split-case 30 hp motors mounted outside the axles of each truck. The lifeguards were Mountain & Gibson 'Simplex' type; sanding gear was by Cummings and the magnetic track brakes by Westinghouse. Hand-operated wheel brakes were also fitted, with a hand-wheel in each vestibule; a second, concentrically-mounted hand-wheel at each end provided a back-up means for applying the magnetic brakes - this was installed in view of the gradients over the Little Orme. Current collection was originally by way of a single trolley pole but this was soon found to be unsatisfactory and was subsequently replaced by two trolleys mounted near the centre of the roof and facing outwards. No further alterations were made to the cars until 1924-5 when the original motors were replaced by more powerful (40 hp) British Thomson-Houston GE249A models with new B49CC controllers, though only one motor (redesignated about this date as BTH249AA) was fitted per bogie; replacement BTH magnetic track brakes were also fitted. In 1931 a programme was started of filling-in one of the side entrances on each end platform, presumably for reasons relating to passenger safety.

At the close of the 1932 summer season Nos. 1-5 were withdrawn and scrapped after all reuseable parts had been removed - including six bogies for use with the ex-Accrington trams (*see below*). In 1936 Nos. 6, 10, 11 and 14 were renumbered to follow on consecutively from the second-hand cars from Accrington and Bournemouth (*see below*) and, although there has been some confusion in the past as to exactly which numbers were taken, it has now been established fairly confidently that they became Nos. 16, 19, 17 and 18 respectively. (It should be pointed out that any stock renumbering on the LCBER was by no means an instantaneous affair and it was not unknown for two cars with the same number to be operating together for a while.) The remaining cars of the batch (i.e. original Nos. 7, 8, 9, 12 and 13) were then all withdrawn and scrapped with the lower saloon of one of them being cut in half to make two shelters for the tram stops at Bryn-y-Bia Road and the Little Orme Café at the bottom of Penrhyn Hill on the Colwyn side. Of the quartet of survivors, No. 19 was earmarked for conversion to a toastrack vehicle for summer use and was reduced to its steel frame and floor, but was finally stripped and scrapped in 1937 (one report says 1941) after the conversion had been deemed impracticable, with some parts being kept in the depot - presumably as spares for the other cars - until at least 1943; No. 16 was scrapped after being damaged by fire in 1945 (*see Chapter Six*) while Nos. 17 and 18 survived until the closure in 1956, though by this time No. 17 was out of use. Final modifications to these cars included the installation of lifeguards between the trucks and the permanent closing of the eight drop windows on each side.

(When it is stated that a tram was scrapped it should be understood that it was the normal practice to strip it first of all parts that had any resale value, or could be used as spares - hence the survival of a wide variety of relics from the LCBER cars, especially those gathered by the Llandudno & Colwyn Bay Tramway Society, museums and private individuals or, remarkably, still carrying out their original functions on another line as detailed in *Appendix Three*.)

Original Cars Nos. 15-18

Known variously as 'Yankees' or 'winter cars' - their reduced capacity and enclosed bodywork protecting the drivers made them suitable for that season's workings - the second batch of cars ordered for the tramway was built in 1909 and delivered in September that year by the United Electric Car Co. Ltd of Preston. Running gear was again by Mountain & Gibson. The bodywork was unique for this country (but not on cars built here for export): a main saloon with eight drop windows each side, fully-vestibuled end platforms each with a seat for two passengers on the closed side opposite the entrance, and a monitor roof supporting a single trolley pole. In view of their design it is possible that these cars were originally destined for an overseas tramway - accounting for the 'Yankee' appellation - but the order was cancelled. Sliding doors gave access to the saloon from the end platforms; one end of the saloon was partitioned-off to provide a smokers' compartment. The deep windows allowed a welcome through flow of air in the summer and accounted for the manufacturer's model name: the 'Preston Patent Semi Convertible Motor Car'. (The basic car could be

A postcard view, probably of the 1930s, of one of the soon to be withdrawn 'Yankees' at the bottom of Penrhyn Hill, heading for Colwyn Bay.   *Author's Collection*

A very weather-beaten No. 17 of 1909 heads towards Colwyn Bay along Rhos Promenade, pursued by No. 12 of 1907, sometime during the 1920s.

Courtesy Llandudno & Colwyn Bay Tramway Society

supplied entirely or partially open or closed as desired by the operator.) Principal dimensions were as follows:

Length of body: over corner posts	20 ft	11in.
Length of body: over platforms	30 ft	1 in.
Length overall	31 ft	1 in.
Width: over pillars	6 ft	3 in.
Width: over roof	6 ft	6 in.
Height: clear inside at centre	7 ft	10 in.
Height: from rail to trolley base	10 ft	11 in.

Running gear consisted of a single four-wheel radial Wartner truck of 10 ft wheelbase, fitted with two Bruce Peebles motors (type unknown) and equipped with rheostatic and manually-operated wheel brakes. In 1927 all four cars were updated with the fitting of Peckham P35 trucks with 40 hp BTH 502FS motors from Brush, new BTH control equipment (BTH B510 type) and the addition of magnetic brakes.

All four cars were withdrawn at the same time, in the winter of 1936 following the arrival of the ex-Bournemouth cars, and stored in the open next to the depot until 1941 when the trucks were removed and sold to Leeds Corporation's Transport Department; there they were used under enclosed double-deck cars Nos. 104, 108, 110 and 433 after regauging to 4 ft 8½ in. Their bodies were subsequently disposed of: two of them went to an army camp at Rhyl and and the other two to a similar establishment nearby at Bodelwyddan, presumably to serve as huts or shelters of some kind until they simply rotted away, their fate unrecorded.

Beside Rhos depot, probably in the late 1930s, with three of the 'Yankees' literally in line to be dismantled. On the left is the roof of a 1907 car. *D.W.K. Jones*

Toastrack No. 20, body and bogies united just after delivery to the tramway.

Original Cars Nos. 19-22

The final four cars ordered for the tramway as new came in 1920 from the English Electric Co. Ltd of Preston, the successor concern to the United Electric Car Co. Ltd. They were identical, completely open toastrack cars each fitted with two English Electric (Mountain & Gibson pattern) equal-wheel bogie trucks. Each truck was powered by a BTH GE249 motor; control was by B18 DD controllers with hand-operated wheel and magnetic braking systems. The end lifeguards were of a fixed type somewhat reminiscent of railway cowcatchers. Seating was for 60 arranged down the car thus: seven lift-over bench seats, a half-width lift-over bench seat each side of the central trolley standard, then seven more lift-over bench seats; the full-width seats held four passengers each and the half-width seats two. (By 1914, when the cars were ordered, the popularity of toastracks on seaside tramways both horse and electric had been demonstrated widely for many years - they had been running on the Isle of Man, for example, since the mid-1880s - so it is somewhat puzzling that the LCBER waited so long before introducing this type of vehicle.)

In 1936, with the renumbering of the 1907 cars Nos. 6, 10, 11 and 14, toastrack 19 was temporarily renumbered 23 for a brief period until the original No. 10, now renumbered 19, was officially withrawn the following year. In 1954 Nos. 19 and 20 were fitted with 'K4' controllers obtained ex-Sunderland, with all four toastracks being scrapped two years later after the closure of the tramway (though several of their seats remained in Wales, to serve as station benches on the 15 in. gauge miniature Fairbourne Railway on the coast of Cardigan Bay, just south of Barmouth).

Second-hand Cars Nos. 1-5

These five cars were ex-Accrington Corporation bogie single-deckers built by Brush in 1915 and 1920, purchased by the LCBER in 1932-3 as replacements for its original Nos. 1-5, taking their old numbers. Their Accrington numbers were 28-32 respectively with Nos. 29 and 32 bought as complete cars, which consequently entered service first as Nos. 2 and 5. In the case of the other three cars only the bodies were acquired, these then being mounted on the six best-condition Mountain & Gibson trucks salvaged from the withdrawn Nos. 1-5 to save the expense and trouble of buying and regauging more Accrington trucks than was strictly necessary. (The Accrington system had a 4 ft track gauge.) Those bogies regauged on Nos. 29 and 32 were Brush type 'C' maximum-traction trucks equipped with one 40 hp Dick, Kerr '30B' motor each. Controllers were Dick, Kerr type 'DB1' 'K4'. (One eye-witness recollection is that the third car put into service, Accrington No. 30, was definitely renumbered 11 until the replacement Nos. 1 and 4 were ready, when it became No. 3. If this was the case, did the original No. 3 assume the original - and worn-out - No. 11's identity for a short while until renumbered 17 in turn?)

The car bodies were of the closed, saloon pattern with one entrance on each vestibuled end platform, with the saloon - accessed via a sliding door at each end - seating 40 passengers on two longitudinal wooden benches. A single

A pair of toastracks: Nos. 22 and 23, the latter car bearing its short-lived 1936 fleet number.

D.W.K. Jones

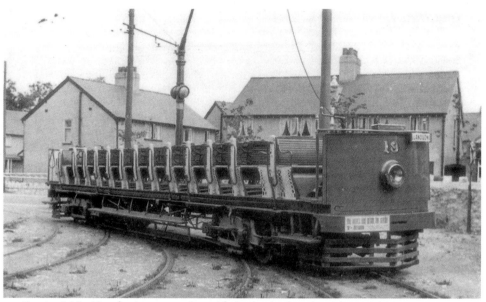

Toastrack No. 19 at the depot, complete with destination board and fares sticker.
Peter Johnson Collection

An unidentified toastrack outside the depot, the car apparently being used for a special working.
D.W.K. Jones

Four views of toastrack No. 21, starting with a shot of it in service on the toll road...

D.W.K. Jones

...and awaiting passengers at the West Shore.   *D.W.K. Jones*

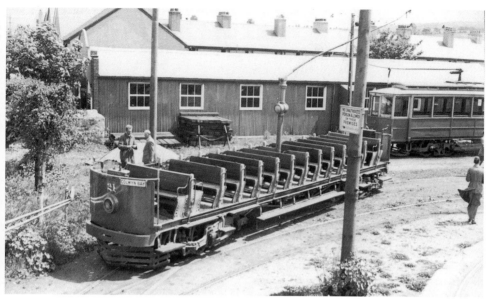

No. 21 outside the depot on 21st May, 1951 with footboards in the boarding position.

D.W.K. Jones

Toastrack No. 21 again at the West Shore on 21st May, 1951 on the Light Railway Transport League special.

D.W.K. Jones

Toastrack No. 20 at the West Shore terminus on 11th August, 1955, loaded for departure.

John Edgington

Another crowded toastrack: this time No. 22, on the same day, leaving the toll road on its way to Colwyn Bay, with another toastrack waiting to enter the single-track section.

John Edgington

Ex-Accrington car No. 2 awaiting passengers at the West Shore terminus. *Author's Collection*

One of the Brush maximum traction trucks as fitted to car No. 2 (ex-Accrington). *D.W.K. Jones*

Ex-Accrington No. 5, seen here at Gloddaeth Street on 11th August, 1955.

John Edgington

Ex-Accrington No. 5 again, seen here together with sister car No. 3 at Rhos depot.

D.W.K. Jones

The empty interior of No. 5 (ex-Accrington) with its padded longitudinal seats and its hanging straps for standing passengers.

D.W.K. Jones

trolley pole was mounted centrally on the monitor roof, and both hand-operated wheel and magnetic brakes were fitted.

During their new life at Llandudno the cars were subjected to several minor alterations, beginning with the immediate removal of their destination indicator boxes and roof-mounted headlights; the latter were replaced with ones from the withdrawn cars, fitted in the standard LCBER position in the centre of the dashes, and the former by boards above the side windows giving the route. Longer roof boards were also fitted, to carry advertisements. By 1936 their Accrington red and cream livery had been replaced by the green and cream of Llandudno; two years later the original seats were removed and rattan ones from the withdrawn cars fitted in their place. In 1952-3 all five cars were equipped with self-aligning trolley-heads bought as spares from Birmingham and - a touch of modern comfort - with Dunlopillo seat cushions from the same source. No. 5 also had a change of motors, the new ones coming from the ex-Bournemouth cars (*see below*).

All five cars survived until 1956, with Nos. 3-5 lasting until the end and Nos. 1 and 2 being scrapped in early January; No. 3 had the distinction of being the last LCBER tram to be overhauled and repainted (in 1952/3).

It should be noted here that the LCBER's car renumbering policy was not as straightforward as might so far appear. The customary tramway practice in such situations was either to allocate second-hand purchases new numbers at the end of the existing fleet list if they simply enlarged it or, if they were intended as replacement vehicles, to give them the numbers of the withdrawn cars. In the case of the LCBER however a hybrid policy was formulated whereby the first five second-hand vehicles took the numbers 1-5 and the next 10 then extended that list (i.e. 6, 7, etc.), regardless of whether or not the original cars of that number had been withdrawn; if they had not, then the original cars were renumbered at the end of this new list. With the arrival of the last two second-hand cars though, this policy was abandoned and they were allocated numbers at the end of the original fleet list.

Second-hand Cars Nos. 6-15

The second batch of second-hand cars was acquired from Bournemouth Corporation in 1936 and was a rather mixed lot in all, comprising 10 passenger cars and one works car (*see later*); the passenger cars were of two separate designs though all were standard open-top, double-deck bogie vehicles built for 3 ft 6 in. gauge operation.

The first design was represented by No. 6 (Bournemouth 85), built by United Electric in 1914. It had elliptically-shaped end platforms, to which vestibules had been added in 1920 to protect the driver from the elements. The bogies were Brill 22E maximum-traction trucks with a Westinghouse W226N motor in each, giving a total of 80 hp. Other electrical equipment was also by Westinghouse while the lifeguards were by Hudson-Browning. Three braking systems were fitted: hand-operated wheel and track brakes, and magnetic. After arriving at Rhos depot their motors were replaced with the LCBER's favourite BTH GE249As, these in turn being replaced in 1953 by two of the batch of Dick, Kerr

Open-topper No. 6 just arrived at the West Shore terminus on 11th August, 1955, with passengers still disembarking.   *John Edgington*

No. 6 again on the same day, this time loading at Colwyn Bay.   *John Edgington*

No. 6 again, this time arriving at Llandudno.   *D.W.K. Jones*

Another ex-Bournemouth car, No. 7, rounding Hooson's Corner.   *D.W.K. Jones*

An ex-Bournemouth car again, this time at the eastern entrance to the toll road, with the toll booth on the right.   *D.W.K. Jones*

A fine, close-up view of open-topper No. 12 at the West Shore terminus.   *D.W.K. Jones*

Open-topper No. 14 loading in Penrhyn Avenue on the last day of public service, its passengers suitably garbed against the elements. *Vic Bradley*

No. 14 again, at the top of Penrhyn Hill in earlier days. Note the wartime masked headlamp - and the missing upper deck one. *D.W.K. Jones*

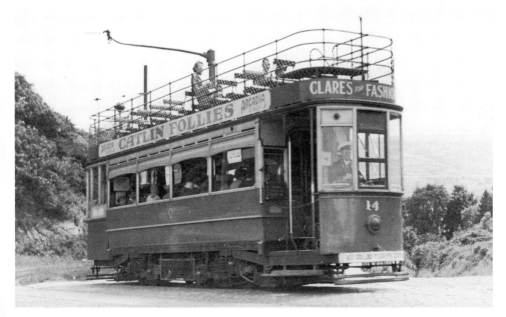

Four more photographs of the ex-Bournemouth cars at work: in Colwyn Bay...

Provenance Unknown

...on the sea-damaged toll road...

D.W.K. Jones

...in Colwyn Bay again... *Provenance Unknown*

...and, finally, in Llandudno. *Provenance Unknown*

Double-decker No. 6 at the West Shore, on a cold-looking 13th October, 1940.

Peter Johnson Collection

Double-decker No. 7 in Colwyn Bay on 11th August, 1955, having just crossed Brompton Avenue railway bridge. *John Edgington*

One of the Brill maximum traction trucks as fitted to open-topper No. 6. *D.W.K. Jones*

The driver's controls of ex-Bournemouth car No. 6 - note the distinctive Westinghouse controller - showing the large controller handle in the 'off' position, the smaller forward/reverse key and the track brake wheel topped by the wheel brake handle. *D.W.K. Jones*

Brompton Avenue railway bridge again, this time with No. 24 crossing.   *D.W.K. Jones*

type '30B' 40 hp motors obtained from Birmingham that year along with their accompanying gears, wheels and axles. (The Birmingham system was also a 3 ft 6 in. gauge one.) This car remained in service to the closure and, as described in Chapter Eight, has by good fortune been preserved.

The second design was made up of two groups in terms of age. All were from Brush, the older group being built in 1921 and numbered on the LCBER (Bournemouth numbers in brackets): 9 (108), 10 (103), 11 (95) and 13 (112). They were similar to No. 6 in overall design but with slightly longer, semi-circular vestibuled end platforms. The trucks were also Brill 22Es but with BTH 'B49' motors and 'B49CC' controllers. Again the motors developed 40 hp, the same as their BTH 'GE249A' replacements. Braking systems were the same as those on No. 6; in 1953 all were fitted with ex-Birmingham motors, gears and wheelsets too. Nos. 9 and 10 were scrapped in January 1956 after involvement in a collision while Nos. 11 and 13 survived until the closure in March.

The younger group comprised five cars built between 1924 and 1926 and numbered (Bournemouth numbers in brackets): 7 (115), 8 (116), 12 (128), 14 (121) and 15 (114). Trucks were again Brill '22Es', with Metrovick 40 hp (MV104) motors and Metrovick controllers. Brakes were the same as on the older cars. It is thought that BTH 'GE249A' motors and 'B49CC' controllers were fitted upon arrival and in 1953 Nos. 8, 12 and 15 were re-equipped in a similar manner to Nos. 6, 9, 10, 11 and 13. No. 7 held the dubious honour of being Bournemouth's 'Last Car', while No. 8 was of course later awarded a similar distinction on the LCBER. All five survived until the closure, then went the way of the rest.

More detailed dimensions of these cars are given below:

	No. 6	Nos. 7-15
Wheelbase: bogie	4 ft 0 in.	4 ft 0 in.
Wheelbase: total	20 ft 0 in.	20 ft 0 in.
Length: over body	23 ft 6 in.	23 ft 6 in.
Length: overall	35 ft 6 in.	36 ft 6 in.
Width	6 ft 4 in.	6 ft 4 in.
Seating: upper deck	32	38
Seating: lower deck	30	30

Second-hand Cars Nos. 23 and 24

The last two cars acquired by the LCBER were ex-Darwen Nos. 24 and 23, renumbered 23 and 24 respectively at Llandudno at the end of the existing number sequence; the reason why they did not retain their coincidentally apt Darwen numbers is because their identities became confused during the lengthy delay in the depot between when they were repainted and when the appropriate transfers were applied (their old numbers not having been marked on them in accordance with usual paint shop practice). They were identical enclosed, double-deck bogie tramcars built in 1936 by the English Electric Co. Ltd of Preston, successor concern to United Electric, as a much smaller, reduced-width version of a modern-looking standard gauge design developed

A good side-on view of one of the ex-Darwen cars, its low ground clearance evident even when unladen.   *Author's Collection*

The lower saloon interior of No. 24, showing the centrally-positioned stairs.   *D.W.K. Jones*

No. 24 at the depot, stickered for the Colwyn Bay shuttle service.   *Author's Collection*

No. 23 holding up the traffic between Rhos and Colwyn Bay, in June 1952.   *H.L. Runnett*

'Spiv' No. 24 again, on the Colwyn Bay shuttle service, this time at the terminal stub.

D.W.K. Jones

1933-5 for Blackpool's tramways (one variant being the famous 'Balloons'). At Darwen their size and streamlined bodywork earned them the nickname of 'Queens' as a shortened form of 'Queen Marys', the liner of that name having been launched in 1934; at Llandudno their crews had a more derogatory name for them - 'Spivs' - on account of their flashy appearance. Though fast (and consequently liked by their drivers), they rode extremely poorly on bad track - and to continue the ocean liner analogy, many passengers complained that their rolling motion induced feelings of sea-sickness! Furthermore, they were also prone to grounding their bodywork on bumpy track, a defect that possibly dated back to June 1936 when, during trials at Darwen, No. 23 (LCBER 24) derailed under a low bridge and the two cars were subsequently modified with, it is believed, smaller wheels.

Entry was via a centre entrance on each side, with a central staircase to the upper deck; a single trolleypole was mounted centrally on the roof. The pair arrived at Llandudno in August 1946 but their testing over the tramway was delayed until late the following year as their English Electric maximum-traction bogie trucks had been sent to Burton-upon-Trent for regauging from 4 ft (which could not have improved the cars' riding). Each car was powered by two 57 hp English Electric motors (type EE305A) and was equipped with English Electric/Dick, Kerr type 'K33' controllers. Other modern refinements included air-powered brakes and hooters.

Each half of the lower saloon held 12 passengers on transverse seats, upholstered in dark red, whilst the narrower upper saloon held 32 on 2 and 1 transverse seats (the centre aisle changing sides at the top of the stairs). It had been intended that they should form the basis of a whole new fleet at Darwen but they were not a success - they rolled a lot on poor track there - and by March 1945 both were out of service; it seems clear now that the standard gauge design had not been modified sufficiently - for reasons of economy - to suit a narrower gauge system. By the end of that year, however, both had been overhauled, presumably with a view to their sale, and in January 1946 the LCBER put in a firm offer of £400 each for them. On 19th August that year No. 23 left Lancashire by road for Wales, followed four days later by No. 24; the Darwen system closed on 5th October.

As described in Chapter Six, these two cars were prohibited by the Ministry of Transport from working the more exposed central section of the LCBER, their 4 ft gauge-designed superstructure being deemed to make them vunerable to overturning in high winds. Instead, they were put on shuttle services in Llandudno and Colwyn Bay in 1948, though No. 23 was withdrawn from its Llandudno working after only a year as the condition of stretches of track there was so bad that it was having a damaging effect upon the car - and this was despite the service being reduced to cover just Mostyn Street and Mostyn Broadway! Although both were officially withdrawn in 1954, they were the very last cars to be scrapped in 1956 after the closure of the line as the company entertained hopes of being able to sell them (but to whom?).

More detailed dimensions are given below:

Length overall	35 ft	6 in.
Width	6 ft	7½ in.
Height: rail to trolley plank	14 ft	8in.
Wheelbase	4 ft	6 in.

Livery

The company's basic livery adopted for the original 1907 cars was maroon below the waist and cream above, fully lined-out in gold. Nos. 1-14 had the legend LLANDUDNO & COLWYN BAY in gold in the centre of the waist panels on each side whilst the car number was painted in gold above the electric headlight in the centre of each dash. The 1909 cars Nos. 15-18 were finished slightly differently, in that they carried the legend LLANDUDNO & COLWYN BAY ELECTRIC RAILWAY LIMITED along the whole length of the rocker panel on each side, with the car number repeated on both sides of the dash headlights.

As a consequence of restrictions on paint supply, during World War I Nos. 1-14 were painted battleship grey as a temporary measure - though some of them continued to sport this colour until they were withdrawn, or repainted in the new official livery of green and cream in 1933 (as were the other original cars); this was basically green panels, cream framing, dark orange roofs, dark brown underframes, red oxide trucks and lifeguards, and black fenders. Gold numbers were carried above the headlight in the centre of each dash with the company crest displayed centrally on each side of the body replacing the original title lettering.

The ex-Bournemouth cars were, according to reliable sources, repainted in LCBER livery before they left the south coast, though the second-hand Accrington cars were re-liveried in their new colours as and when they needed a repaint, not at the time they arrived on the tramway, thereby presenting something of a colourful confusion on the streets! Nos. 23 and 24 were painted in green and cream, this time in flowing bands with the two colours separated by black lining. (See the accompanying photographs for the exact pattern used.)

Indicators

The original Nos. 1-14 were equipped, as delivered, with destination boards hung at the bottom of the windows in the centre of each side and end of the car. Later, in line with the company's standard policy, roof boards were added on each side giving details of the complete route travelled; in 1931 the front boards were moved to the nearside front window at each end. Original cars 15-18 as delivered had a destination box mounted on the roof at each end but these too were removed and replaced by route boards on each side, again with a metal destination sign in the nearside front window. The toastracks simply had one of these signs hung on the front dash when running.

During World War II the cars' indicators disappeared entirely, presumably as a security measure akin to the wholesale removal of road signs, though the metal destination signs were reinstated after the end of hostilities. It was not until the tramway's final years that any others were used (in addition to the metal signs): black-printed yellow paper strips giving terminal and intermediate points, pasted above the windows of the closed cars and on the lower off-side of the dashes of the toastracks.

The second-hand cars purchased before World War II from Accrington and Bournemouth were adapted in line with the above policy in that destination boxes were replaced by metal signs. In the case of the ex-Darwen cars a slightly different arrangement was used: the two destination boxes above the cab windows at each end were fitted with blinds giving (usually for No. 23) the Llandudno terminal points and (usually for No. 24) the Colwyn Bay ones. (The two side destination boxes, one over each entrance, were left blank.)

Works Cars

During its life the LCBER possessed two powered works cars. The first, built by Brush in 1901 or 1902 for the Taunton & West Somerset Electric Railways & Tramways Co. Ltd (later the Taunton Electric Traction Co. Ltd), was an open-top, double-deck, four-wheeled passenger car with a 6 ft 6 in. wheelbase Brush 'A' truck equipped with two Brush 800 17 hp motors and magnetic brakes. In 1905, with the reconstruction of the Taunton system, it was sold along with the other five original cars to the Leamington & Warwick Electric Tramway, opened that year. Here it was numbered (probably) 11 - its Taunton number is unknown - and converted into a scrubber car. In 1930 it moved again (the Balfour, Beatty-owned Leamington line closed that August), this time to Llandudno where it remained in service before becoming, less running gear, a stores shed at the depot.

The tramway'second works car was obtained in 1936 to replace the ex-Leamington vehicle and it possessed a similarly eventful history. It too had begun life in 1901 as an open-top passenger car, in this case Poole & District Electric Traction Co. No. 1 built by G.F. Milnes on a Brill 21E truck equipped with two BTH GE58-6T 28 hp motors. In 1905 it was acquired, along with the Poole system, by Bournemouth Corporation Tramways and renumbered 55. Wheelbase was 6 ft, as was the car's width; length was 16 ft over the body and 27 ft 7 in. overall; the lifeguards were by Tidswell. In 1921, whilst still at Bourrnemouth, it was converted into a rail-grinder and its top deck fittings removed - although a rather peculiar visual effect resulted from the fact that neither staircase was so treated! It came to Llandudno with the other Bournemouth cars purchased in 1936 and was given a plain grey livery, the number 23 and lettered CONSTRUCTION CAR. In 1947, after the arrival of the two ex-Darwen cars, it was renumbered 23A.

In addition to these two cars - both of which ran on 3 ft 6 in. gauge lines throughout their lives - the LCBER is thought to have operated at least four non-powered items of permanent way stock, including a welding unit and a small, plate-frame bogie, for carrying rails, which was obtained from Coventry Corporation in 1941 when that 3 ft 6 in. gauge system closed. (This latter vehicle had been employed in similar fashion at Coventry after beginning life as a bogie under a 1880s Falcon steam trailer there.) These maintenance vehicles were simply towed to wherever needed by a works car (or passenger car pre-1930) and then positioned manually. There were, in addition, at least two four-wheeled trucks - possibly dating from the construction of the line - used to carry

Works car No. 23 (formerly Bournemouth No. 55) complete with its somewhat incongruous staircases, outside the depot.   *D.W.K. Jones*

Works car No. 23 again, this time inside the depot.   *D.W.K. Jones*

sand for the the trams back to the depot (where it could be dried) whilst being pushed or pulled by one of the powered cars. In the early years this sand was collected from the West Shore; it later years it came from Penrhyn Bay when the coastal erosion there made it easier to gather. When not in use these trucks were kept in a 'siding' - probably just a short section of isolated track from which they could be manhandled onto the running line when required - laid in a small quarry carved out of the cliff face on Penrhyn Hill. (The quarry was also used to supply fresh ballast for the reserved sections of the tramway, and probably dated back to the line's construction.)

The tramway's other vital maintenance vehicle was its road-going tower wagon used for servicing the overhead. It is thought the LCBER operated two during its life, a Fordson truck (registration number EUN 148) purchased new in 1948 replacing the original wooden, horse-drawn one.

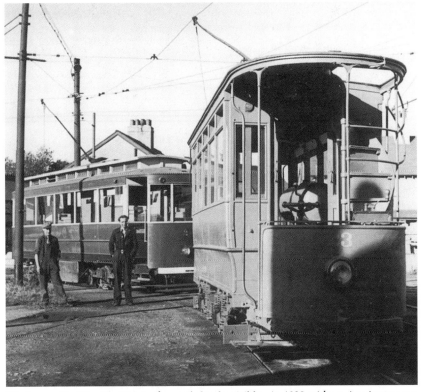

Works car No. 23 - its stairs to the roof clearly visible - in 1938 with ex-Accrington car No. 2 in new LCBER livery behind. *D.W.K. Jones*

An impressive depot line-up in November 1955 with original cars Nos. 17 (ex-11) and 21, and second-hand cars Nos. 2, 4 and 10.   *D.W.K. Jones*

Open-toppers Nos. 12 and 7 and works car No. 23A in the car shed in May 1951, with their trolley poles facing towards the entrance - the normal position adopted for working in and out of the depot.   *D.W.K. Jones*

Fleet List

No.	Built	Builder	Type	Withdrawn	Remarks
Original stock: the closed single-deckers					
1	1907	MRC&W	8wb	1932/3	
2	1907	MRC&W	8wb	1932/3	
3	1907	MRC&W	8wb	1932/3	
4	1907	MRC&W	8wb	1932/3	
5	1907	MRC&W	8wb	1932/3	
6	1907	MRC&W	8wb	1945	Renumbered 16 in 1936
7	1907	MRC&W	8wb	1936	
8	1907	MRC&W	8wb	1936	
9	1907	MRC&W	8wb	1936	
10	1907	MRC&W	8wb	1937	Renumbered 19 in 1936
11	1907	MRC&W	8wb	1956	Renumbered 17 in 1936
12	1907	MRC&W	8wb	1936	
13	1907	MRC&W	8wb	1936	
14	1907	MRC&W	8wb	1956	Renumbered 18 in 1936
15	1909	UEC	4wt	1936	Cut-up 1941
16	1909	UEC	4wt	1936	Cut-up 1941
17	1909	UEC	4wt	1936	Cut-up 1941
18	1909	UEC	4wt	1936	Cut-up 1941
Original stock: the toastracks					
19	1920	EE	8wb	1956	Numbered 23 1936-7
20	1920	EE	8wb	1956	
21	1920	EE	8wb	1956	
22	1920	EE	8wb	1956	
Second-hand stock: the closed single-deckers acquired 1932/3					
1	1915	Brush	8wb	1956	Ex-Accrington 28
2	1915	Brush	8wb	1956	Ex-Accrington 29
3	1915	Brush	8wb	1956	Ex-Accrington 30
4	1920	Brush	8wb	1956	Ex-Accrington 31
5	1920	Brush	8wb	1956	Ex-Accrington 32
Second-hand stock: the open-top double-deckers acquired 1936					
6	1914	UEC	8wb	1956	Ex-Bournemouth 85; preserved
7	1924-26	Brush	8wb	1956	Ex-Bournemouth 115
8	1924-26	Brush	8wb	1956	Ex-Bournemouth 116; official 'Last Car'
9	1921	Brush	8wb	1956	Ex-Bournemouth 108
10	1921	Brush	8wb	1956	Ex-Bournemouth 103
11	1921	Brush	8wb	1956	Ex-Bournemouth 95
12	1924-26	Brush	8wb	1956	Ex-Bournemouth 128
13	1921	Brush	8wb	1956	Ex-Bournemouth 112
14	1924-26	Brush	8wb	1956	Ex-Bournemouth 121
15	1924-26	Brush	8wb	1956	Ex-Bournemouth 114
Second-hand stock: the closed double-deckers acquired 1946					
23	1936	EE	8wb	1954	Ex-Darwen 24; cut-up 1956
24	1936	EE	8wb	1954	Ex-Darwen 23; cut-up 1956
Powered works cars					
--	1901	Brush	4wt	1936	See Chapter Ten
23	1901	Milnes	4wt	1956	Renumbered 23A in 1947; see Chapter Ten

Key
4wt = 4-wheeled truck tramcar, 8wb - 8-wheeled bogie tramcar, Brush - Brush Electrical Engineering Co. Ltd, EE - English Electric Co. Ltd, MRC&W - Midland Railway Carriage & Wagon Co. Ltd, UEC - United Electric Car Co. Ltd.

Ex-Southdown GUF 128 waiting to take over from open-topper No. 6 in March 1956.

D.W.K. Jones

Open-topper No. 6 and ex-East Kent Leyland AJG 26 successor - used for driver training - outside the depot during the tramway's final days.   *D.W.K. Jones*

Fleet List of the Buses

Fleet No.	Reg. No.	Built	Body	Withdrawn	Remarks
Driver training vehicle acquired 1955					
ex-East Kent (Leyland 'Titan' 'TD5' chassis)					
--	AJG 26	1938	Park Royal	1956	
Spare vehicle acquired 1956					
ex-Southdown (Guy 'Arab' '5LW' chassis)					
--	GUF 175	1945	Weymann	-	
Original service vehicles acquired 1956					
ex-Newcastle (Daimler 'CO5G' chassis)					
1	HTN 231	1939	Northern Coach Builders	1961	Converted to open-top 1956
2	HTN 233	1939	Northern Coach Builders	1961	
Original service vehicles acquired 1956					
ex-Southdown (Guy 'Arab' '5LW' chassis)					
3	GUF 128	1945	Northern Counties	1957	
4	GUF 133	1945	Northern Counties	1959	
5	GUF 155	1945	Northern Counties	1957	Rebuilt as breakdown tender
6	GUF 165	1945	Northern Counties	1959	
7	GUF 177	1945	Weymann	1961	
8	GUF 183	1945	Weymann	1961	
9	GUF 387	1945	Weymann	1961	
10	GUF 388	1945	Weymann	1961	
11	GUF 391	1946	Weymann	1961	
12	GUF 393	1946	Weymann	1961	
13	GUF 398	1946	Park Royal	1961	
Replacement service vehicle acquired 1957					
ex-Southdown (Guy 'Arab' '5LW' chassis)					
3	GUF 159	1945	Northern Counties	1961	Converted to open-top 1960
Replacement service vehicles acquired 1959					
ex-East Kent (Guy 'Arab' '5LW' chassis)					
4	BJG 355	1944	Park Royal	1961	
6	BJG 356	1944	Park Royal	1961	

AJG 26 again, outside a depot full of cars awaiting the scrapman's torch.   *D.W.K. Jones*

Appendix Three

The Seaton Connection

The story of the LCBER would not be complete without mention of the connections it has with a tramway that did not even exist when the Llandudno line closed: the Seaton & District Electric Tramway in South Devon, running inland for 3¼ scenic miles beside the River Axe. The beginnings of the tramway are to be found in a 15 in. gauge portable line constructed by Claude W. Lane, a New Barnet engineer and manufacturer of battery-electric delivery vehicles. After three years' operation at fêtes and the like (including trials in 1951 on a semi-permanent line at St Leonard's-on-Sea on the south coast) a permanent site was sought, and in 1952 the line opened as the ¼ mile Voryd Park miniature tramway in Rhyl. The first of the line's two original cars was a one-third scale model of LCBER No. 23, with one centre entrance and a straight staircase for practical reasons; even so, accommodation on the two decks was somewhat cramped! (The line's other car, No. 225 - was a model of a Blackpool prototype.)

In 1953/4 operations - as Modern Electric Tramways Ltd - moved to a bigger site at Eastbourne and rebuilt to a 2 ft gauge, though the Voryd Park tramway continued with another operator and car No. 23 until 1957; in 1958 No. 23 was sold and is now in private ownership. In 1969 the Eastbourne line too closed and the tramway moved to occupy the southern portion of the old London & South Western Railway branch from Seaton Junction to the seaside resort of Seaton, opening in 1970 on the new gauge of 2 ft 9 in. After the tramway went to Eastbourne (and of course again at Seaton) the wider gauge(s) made it possible for new cars to be constructed using equipment obtained from 'full-size' trams. Thus Eastbourne cars Nos. 2, 4, 6, 7 and 12 incorporated (together with parts from other systems' trams) the following items:

No. 2 (built 1964, Eastbourne): parts of LCBER cars used in the construction of bulkheads and sliding doors.

No. 4 (1961 Eastbourne): motorman's air-brake valves, air whistles, controllers and circuit-breakers from the LCBER's ex-Darwen cars.

No. 6 (1954 New Barnet; rebuilt 1956, 1962 and 1989): top deck seats and scrollwork from LCBER No. 8 (ex-Bournemouth); headlamps, gongs, signal-bells and circuit-breakers from various other LCBER cars. Fittingly, this bogie open-topper of freelance design was operated on a short length of track in Bodafon Fields from 4th to 6th May, 1996 as part of the annual Llandudno Transport Festival's commemoration of the 40th anniversary of the LCBER's closure.

No. 7 (1958 New Barnet): top deck seats from the LCBER's ex-Bournemouth cars; headlamps, gongs, signal-bells, circuit-breakers from LCBER cars, and controllers from No. 3 (ex-Accrington).

No. 12 (1966 Eastbourne): the other two controllers from the LCBER's ex-Darwen cars.

All the above cars are still in service on the tramway, which operates a full service during the summer season plus special workings - includings trips for bird watchers, Santa Specials and the like - during the winter months. Full timetable details can be obtained by telephone (01297 20375), email (info@tram.co.uk) or from the tramway's website (www.tram.co.uk)

Appendix Four

Other Tramway Proposals

The LCBER was not of course the only tramway to be built in Llandudno: from 1902 onwards the Great Orme Tramway (GOT) has filled its specialised role of taking visitors (and residents) up the southern slopes of the Great Orme. The history of this cable tramway has been covered comprehensively elsewhere (*see Bibiliography*) and although no other tramways were constructed in either Llandudno or Colwyn Bay, three proposals covering the area deserve mention. The most ambitious of these, reported in the local press in September 1903, was for an electric light railway to link West Kirby on the Wirral with Rhyl, Colwyn Bay and Llandudno. Perhaps not surprisingly, since it would have entailed the construction of a bridge (or more probably a causeway and bridge) at least four miles long across the Dee estuary, nothing more was heard of this scheme.

The second proposal was for a far less ambitious but equally spectacular line. In 1879 a private toll road had been constructed around the headland of the Great Orme for those visitors daring enough to walk or ride from east to west along a road that clung to the very side of the rockface (replacing an even more precipitous footpath carved out two decades before). Built at a cost of £14,000 the Marine Drive, as it was named, was 4 miles 130 yards in length (though the distance between entrance and exit across the landward side of the peninsula was less than 1½ miles) and proved such a success that in 1897 it was purchased by Llandudno UDC for £10,500 from its owner, the Great Orme's Head Marine Drive Co. Ltd.

Even before the road had been opened fully suggestions were being made to replace it with a tramway. One such proposal came from the writer of a letter to the *Caernarvon & Denbigh Herald* of 21st August, 1875 who claimed that the tram fare would be in the region of only 3*d*. compared with the sum of 5*s*. charged by the fly drivers - drivers of light carts - who carried people up and around the rough pathways on the Orme. The suggestion remained just a suggestion for a quarter of a century until, during the protracted birth of the LCBER, Llandudno UDC decided to investigate the matter more fully. The General Purposes Committee submitted a report by the engineer E. Paley Stephenson to the Council in November 1901; the report was a detailed study for what would be known as the Great Orme's Head Marine Drive Tramway. It was to follow the plan of the proposed Llandudno-Colwyn Bay line in that it would be a 3 ft 6 in. gauge electric overhead tramway; on the Marine Drive section of the route from the Happy Valley Lodge on the eastern side of the Orme to the Penmorfa Lodge on the west the line was to run 3 ft from the kerb on the landward side of the road whilst on the town side of the Orme two alternative routes were considered. The first was via Abbey Road, West Parade, Conway Crescent, Gloddaeth Street and North Parade; the second was via Abbey Road, Tudnor Street, Church Walks - later the terminus of the GOT - and North Parade. The first route was the preferred one of the two as an agreement might be made with the Llanduno & Colwyn Bay promoters for common running over this section. The second route, on the other hand, would be the more costly one to build and operate and, passing more houses, was likely to give rise to more opposition from residents.

Construction of the line would have entailed the removal of about 1,350 cubic yards of rock from the Marine Drive as the road was discovered by Stephenson to be narrower than the statutory 16 ft in several places. The cost of construction was estimated at £34,000 for the first route and £35,000 for the second. A 15 minute service was envisaged, running in an anti-clockwise direction around the headland with both open and closed cars, and a fare of 6*d*.

It is tempting to speculate as to whether or not the tramway would still be with us today if it had been built - but it was not, killed as the proposal was by the reluctance of the Council to begin a new tramway venture when it might well be called upon to complete the one already on its doorstep, opposition from the Llandudno Pier Co. who foresaw a possible loss of revenue and, one would imagine, similar opposition from the promoters of the GOT. (The Council did later introduce a motor bus service round the Drive, but not until 1928.) Only one comparable line was ever built in the British Isles: that on the Douglas Head Marine Drive in the Isle of Man - coincidentally just a summer steamer's day trip away from Llandudno. Opened in 1896, its construction doubtless played some part in the minds of the Llandudno Councillors but since it failed to reopen after World War II it is realistic to assume that its Welsh counterpart, like so many other tramways, might well have become a fellow casualty.

The third local tramway proposal was for a much shorter line altogether: along the seashore by the Parade from opposite St George's Hospital at its northern end as far as the Little Orme (a distance of about 1½ miles). The idea was put to the Local Board in November 1892 but was turned down. Curiously, although the line was to be worked by electricity rather than horses, it was to be laid on the beach next to Parade, not on the roadway - presumably the intention was that such a siting of the line would result in no inconvenience to the resort's promenaders, thus making the proposal more attractive; the ploy, however, was unsuccessful, despite the promoters' promise to install electric lighting on the Parade if permission for the tramway were to be granted.

Acknowledgements

This book could not have been written without the help afforded me by many people over more than 30 years of researching the story of the LCBER and it would be impossible, without fear of embarrassing oversight, to list all those who have helped me in so many ways during that time; so to everyone who did - thank you. I am especially grateful to those individuals who kindly shared their memories of the working tramway with me, notably R.C. Anderson, F.P. Groves, E.N.C. Haywood, R.B. Mayoh and Bernard J. Norgate; special thanks also go to Margaret Donnison for assisting with the photographs and drawing the maps. I should also like to thank the staff of the National Library of Wales, of the Library of the University College of North Wales Bangor, and of Llandudno, Birmingham and Cambridge public libraries for all their patient assistance with my attempts to unearth long-hidden facts and figures.

Information regarding the Llandudno & Colwyn Bay Tramway Society - to the members and officials of which an immense debt of gratitude is owed for their role in keeping the memory of the the LCBER alive - can be obtained from the Membership Secretary, Kath Sutton, at 3 Pine Grove, Rhos-on-Sea, Colwyn Bay LL28 4LW.

Bibliography

Anderson, R.C., *A History of Crosville Motor Services*, David & Charles, 1981.

A History of the Llandudno & Colwyn Bay Electric Railway Limited, Quail Map Co., Exeter, 1968, reprinted 1970 with minor corrections.

Crosland-Taylor, W.J. *Crosville: The Sowing and the Harvest*, Littlebury Bros, Liverpool, 1948; 2nd ed. Transport Publishing Co., 1987.

Jay, David & Voice, David, *Next Stop Seaton!* Adam Gordon, Brora, 2003.

Lawson, R. & Morris, G.C.J., *The Llandudno & Colwyn Bay Electric Railway*, Light Railway Transport League, 1956.

Martin, Brian P. (editor), *Trams...a nostalgic look back*, Llandudno Tramway Society.

Price, Geoff, *Trams leave here for Llandudno and Colwyn Bay*, Pride Books, Carnforth, 1983.

A Nostalgic Look at Llandudno & Colwyn Bay Trams Since 1945, Silver Link Publishing, Peterborough, 1997.

Rivers, Stuart (ed.), *The Last Tram to Colwyn Bay*, Llandudno & Colwyn Bay Tramway Society, 2006.

Smith, Peter M., *Llandudno & Colwyn Bay Electric Railway in the 1920s*, Llandudno & Colwyn Bay Electric Railway Society.

Tucker, N., *Colwyn Bay: its origin and growth*, Colwyn Bay Borough Council, 1953.

Turner, Keith, *North Wales Tramways*, David & Charles, 1979.

The Great Orme Tramway - over a century of service, Gwasg Carreg Gwalch, Llanrwst, 2003.

Trams Beside the Seaside - the story of the Llandudno & Colwyn Bay Electric Railway, Gwasg Carreg Gwalch, Llanrwst, 2004.

Other printed sources consulted include appropriate trade directories and journals, transport history journals, local newspapers, relevant statutory instruments, reports of the Light Railway Commissioners, official returns, Ordnance Survey maps and sundry items of ephemeral material relating to the background, setting and history of the LCBER.

Index

Abergele, 33
Accidents, 111, 143
Balfour, Beatty & Co. Ltd, 47, 63
Bodelwyddan, 121
British Electric Traction Co. Ltd, 23
Buses,
  Crosville, 27, 63, 67, 81, 89, 93, 95
  LCBER, 57, 63, 79, 81, 91, 93, 95, 155
  Other, 57, 63
Caernarvonshire Electric Traction
  Syndicate Ltd, 17
Cayley, Sir George, 11, 14, 15
Conwy, 42
Damage,
  By fire, 67, 119
  By sea, 67, 71, 75
Deganwy, 10, 27, 43, 53
Electricity supply, 23, 65, 81
Fares, 105, 111
Hamilton, W.G., 65
Hewitt & Rhodes, 15
Horse-drawn carriages, 101, 157
Indicators, 133, 148, 149
Light Railway & General Construction Co.
  Ltd, 10
Light Railway Orders, 9 *et seq.*, 43, 51 *et
  seq.*, 81, 101, 105
Livery, 133, 148, 149
Llandudno & Colwyn Bay Electric
  Railway Ltd, 47 *et seq.*
Llandudno & Colwyn Bay Electric
  Traction Co. Ltd, 15
Llandudno & Colwyn Bay Tramway
  Society, 5, 100, 119
Llandudno & District Electric Tramways
  Construction Co. Ltd, 17, 43, 47
Llandudno, Colwyn Bay & Rhyl Electric
  Traction Co. Ltd, 11
Llandudno Pier Co., 158
Llandudno Tramway Society, 100
Marine Drive, 157
Modern Electric Tramways Ltd, 156
Moorhouse, W.H., 23
Mostyn family, 7, 11
Museum of British Transport, 93, 100
Nail, Sir Joseph, 63, 75, 79
Parry, J.P.M., & Associates Ltd, 100
Peebles, Bruce, & Co. Ltd, 17, 23, 52, 113,
  121

Railways,
  Fairbourne Railway, 123
  London & North Western Railway, 9,
    10, 11, 23, 33
  London & South Western Railway, 156
  Talyllyn Railway, 79, 97
Rhyl, 11, 14, 93, 121, 156, 157
Sellon, Stephen, 17, 23, 47
Services, 26, 53, 63, 67, 68, 71, 75, 81, 101,
  105, 147
Strikes, 57
Tolls, 111
Tramways,
  Accrington, 63 *et seq.*
  Barnsley, 23
  Birmingham 71, 133, 143
  Blackpool, 97, 143
  Bournemouth, 63 *et seq.*
  Canvey Island, 17, 113
  Cheltenham, 63
  Coventry, 149
  Darwen, 67 *et seq.*
  Delhi, 63
  Great Orme Tramway, 5, 9, 79, 97, 157,
    158
  Isle of Man, 123, 158
  Leamington & Warwick, 63, 149
  Leeds, 121
  Mansfield, 63
  Northampton, 100
  Notts & Derbys, 63
  Poole, 149
  Rhyl, 156
  St Leonard's-on-Sea, 156
  Seaton, 156
  Stockport, 71
  Sunderland, 71, 123
  Taunton, 149
  Tynemouth, 23
Tramway Museum Society, 93
Tramways Extension Syndicate, 17
Trolleybuses, 63
von Donop, Lieut-Col P.G., 17, 23
Walter & Co., 93
Welsh Traction Co. Ltd, 14, 17
West Kirby, 157
World War I, 27, 53, 57, 65, 113, 148
World War II, 65, 67, 71, 105, 148, 149, 158